MW00775581

MEN ARE FINDERS, Women are Choosers

YOUR BIBLICAL GUIDE to Discovering DIVINE RELATIONSHIP

BYRON P. FRANKLIN, SR.

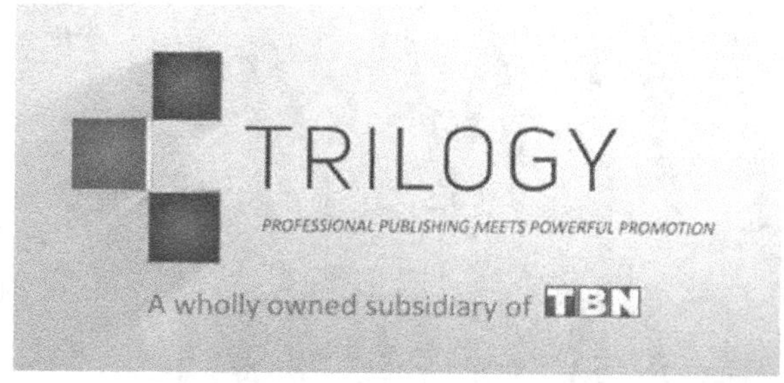

Trilogy Christian Publishers
A Wholly Owned Subsidiary of Trinity Broadcasting Network
2442 Michelle Drive | Tustin, CA 92780

Copyright © 2018 by Byron P. Franklin, Sr.

All Scripture quotations, unless otherwise noted, taken from THE HOLY BIBLE, NEW INTERNATIONAL VERSION®, NIV® Copyright © 1973, 1978, 1984, 2011 by Biblica, Inc.® Used by permission. All rights reserved worldwide.

Scripture quotations marked (KJV) taken from The Holy Bible, King James Version. Cambridge Edition: 1769.

All rights reserved, including the right to reproduce this book or portions thereof in any form whatsoever.

For information, address Trilogy Christian Publishing
Rights Department, 2442 Michelle Drive, Tustin, Ca 92780.
Trilogy Christian Publishing/ TBN and colophon are trademarks of Trinity Broadcasting Network.

For information about special discounts for bulk purchases, please contact Trilogy Christian Publishing.

Manufactured in the United States of America
10 9 8 7 6 5 4 3 2 1
Library of Congress Cataloging-in-Publication Data is available.
ISBN 978-1-64088-063-4
ISBN 978-1-64088-064-1 (ebook)

MEN ARE FINDERS, Women are Choosers

YOUR BIBLICAL GUIDE to *Discovering* DIVINE RELATIONSHIP

BYRON P. FRANKLIN, SR.

INTRODUCTION

I read an article somewhere the other day that made a point that we should stop listening to people who claim to be relationship experts, simply because they are celebrities. It seems now-a-days that all you need is a TV show or 20 minutes of fame, and you can transition right over into telling people how to live their lives. The truth is that many of those giving relationship advice are fresh out of troubled relationships themselves. It is a sad reality that most people are so hungry for a better life that they will take advice from almost anyone. The problem with this approach is that success in one area doesn't always equal success in another. Many times, those giving advice can be more concerned with financial gain than genuine care for others.

I'm pretty sure that most people have a sincere desire to be in a happy, loving and caring relationship. And most desire to walk through this journey of life together with someone who is committed and loyal, and with whom they can do the same. It's a strange truth, however, that people would listen to a so-called star but totally avoid the idea that God Himself could guide them to a divinely designed great relationship. God is a God of purpose, and in His Kingdom everything about your life is connected in some way to His plan. For those who haven't developed a personal relationship with the Lord, this is just one of the benefits of doing so. When you connect to something that has already been designed, all you must do is discover your purpose and walk it out. Everything you will ever need in life has already been provided for along the path God has laid out for your life. You will see as you read through my story that I have discovered that it is a whole lot easier to follow God's pre-set plan than to make up your own.

My process to happiness started out no differently than most people's you see or hear about on television or social media. The difference with me is that I'm not what most would consider famous. I'm not writing this book as an attempt to squeeze a few bucks out of a flash with fame. I started writing this book almost 16 years ago as a sort of journal of my transformation from brokenness to wholeness. This book details the process that led me to my wife, Meriam, and our marriage is still going strong nearly 19 years later.

When I met my wife, I had been recently called into the ministry. I began writing and teaching lessons God was showing me to singles as kind of guide on the dating process. What I did not know at the time was that God was laying the groundwork for the process that would direct me to find my wife. Once I realized what God had given me, I felt I had to capture the process for others, and so I began the process of recording and structuring the principles I learned into book format so that others can learn and apply them in their own lives. Over the years, I have progressed from ministering primarily to singles to now serving as senior pastor of a church for more than 13 years. In the process, I have had the opportunity to counsel many people both single and married, which has helped to develop my understanding of the importance of following God's direction in the process of finding and choosing a spouse.

What I want you to know as you read this book and decide if the lessons outlined are for you is 1) my heart from the very beginning is in the right place, because this information began with you in mind and 2) this story must have something that the devil does not want you to get because of the constant opposition I've had while writing. If this book can help anyone cross over to a place of trusting God to help find or choose a God directed relationship, then I've done my job. I've discovered that there's only one true relationship expert, and that expert is God.

Years ago, I had a football teammate who used to say, "No man alive can cover me one-on-one." He was a unique blend of tailback and wide receiver. He was a true running back with wide receiver hands. Because of his uniqueness, it made him an expert at what he did. Yet I'm pretty sure that there is no human alive that has perfected relationships, or even the process for getting into a good one. But because of God's uniqueness, He's the expert on life in every area. This book is about a God-directed process of getting those who desire to have the right relationship the best chance for success.

Of course, you can do websites, meet and greet sessions, blind dates and all the modern stuff that "might" work, but at the end of the day you need better guidelines to go by. If you are reading this book, there's a great chance that you are tired of the same old results you've been getting with your relational life, and you want something different to happen. If you keep having the same results, it may be because you keep using the same process. It's an old saying but so true, "*If you always do what you have always done, you will always get what you have always gotten.*" I'm not sure who said it first, but it's hard to argue. I must warn you, however, that although this is geared toward you recognizing someone who is for you, it will also challenge you to really take a good look at yourself. This book could very well be an introduction to a new you.

So, this will be my story of the discovery that got me to where I am today. It is time tested and, even better, it's life tested. If you're single, I'm sure you'll get at least one thing out of my story and instruction that will make you think about how you are going about the process of starting relationships. You are either one of two types of people. You are either reading this book because you're just interested in whatever you can find to be better prepared for a relationship, or you're like many of us in life who have been in a struggle to get this thing right. Any successful project must have a good foundation, so let this book be a part of your good foundation that directs you to your desire for a great relationship. This information can also help guide you toward the journey into purpose and being fulfilled. Please understand, relationships are challenging, even the good ones. We need God to help us because of the ongoing, never ending process of growing up.

Some people get to a place in life and decide to never grow beyond their point of comfort, and others decide to treat life as a journey and never look to settle for life where it is. First, you need to know which one of these two people you are and then learn which one of these two people the other person is as well. The recognition of which person you are is not about exterior appearances or how much money a person has in their account, but it's more about the quality of a person's spirit and a drive to want more. If you're the type of person that's going somewhere in life, you would never be fulfilled with someone who wants to just stay where they are for the rest of their lives and accept whatever happens.

My wife made an awesome observation while speaking to our pastor the other day. She said, "God places a spirit of drive in some men and women that will never allow them to settle in where they are." This particular drive that He gives is not a spirit of being ungrateful, but it is a drive to find more of life in God and to see more of what his power can manifest in the life of this generation. If that drive is a part of who you are, then it would be a very challenging relationship to not have someone that does not have or even understands that. This is just one small aspect of understanding what you should be looking for in the process of discovering whom you should have by your side. This is not about ministry, *per se*, but it is about life. Your life is your ministry.

It's funny that my wife and I are so balanced even in being totally different. I have ideas that are about 10,000 miles high, and she reaches up and brings them and me back down to about 1000 feet. And sometimes she just lets them float away. Then there are times when I bring us both up to 10,000 miles. The point is, we work well together. We've done great things in the body of Christ in the last 15 years together as a team. I shared with her just the other day that I felt that in some ways we've done a better job in our teamwork role on outside Kingdom projects than we're doing in the home for ourselves. My point in that statement was that I want us to challenge ourselves to make sure we get the full benefit of what God has done in bringing us together at home, too. Sometimes we in ministry overlook our homes and focus on the Kingdom goals and forget that the benefit should work for us even more so at home. Our lives together are fruitful, but it's not the total blessing until it's a blessing in and out of our house. I believe that ministry work should be a blessing to others without it costing you your family and your joy and happiness. That's for those who are in or headed to ministry. I just wanted to give a shout out to those who are being called to the world of ministry.

Moving back to why we're here…

You know how you buy a new car, and before you bought that car you had no idea that there were so many of that type of car on the road? It's as if they were all invisible until you got yours home, then all of a sudden that car started popping up everywhere. The voice of God becoming alive in my spiritual ears is what happened to me when I began hearing God's voice directing me in my life. Once the door was opened to me hearing His voice, I began to see and hear things that I never realized were there.

There was one major decision made in my thinking that placed me in the mindset for this awakening to occur in my life. I had decided that I didn't want to do or have anything going forward in my life unless I was sure that it was from God. I was serious about that! No job, business or especially any relationship. I had made a mess of things in my life, and I knew I had to look outside myself to get it back together. I'm very thankful today that my life has been transformed.

One great point to know, however, is that I'm not going to say that it was God sending me through a hard time to get me to this greater place in my life now. I did go through a hard place. God knew it was going to happen, He helped me through it, and I'm in a much better place now. But the truth is, I made a bunch of bad decisions leading me into a downward spiral that many people never recover from.

First, I was ready to own my mistakes. You will need to be honest as well. You must also be ready to move forward with your life. There are some things in your life today that cannot go into your future. It could be people, it could be past experiences, and most of all, it could be your thinking. In baseball, you will never get to second base with one foot on first base. As we go through my story, you'll find that there was a lot of work and years of time with God and myself ahead. Why don't you do the same? Let's just start the process of looking into who you are and why you made some of the decisions you made that took you through the challenges that led you on this search. I know believe that you desire to find the right person that God has for you, and based on my experience, that "can" happen and God will help you.

THE POWER TO CHOOSE

In all that we have been blessed with as human beings, whether in the body of Christ or outside the body, the greatest blessing is the power to choose. The power to make decisions to go in whatever direction we decide gives us the ultimate control in our lives but that ultimate control also gives us ultimate responsibility. To whom much is given, much is required.

In that choice to decide we see a God who loves us enough NOT to control us but a Creator who seeks companionship out of desire, not conditions or acts of validation through performance, but simply for the relationship. Not for gifts but for the intimacy. "He wants us to want Him for Him."

1. You have a choice to be saved under the plan God established in His Word.
2. You have a choice to decide to go your own way in Life under your own plan.
3. You have a choice to choose whatever you want.

There are benefits to following God's instruction and painful losses for choosing another direction. This can't be any more evident in any area greater than the area of relationships. Throughout time marriage and dating has and continues to be a challenge and I know it's not the will of God that we struggle in this area, after all marriage and relationships between man and women was His idea. I like many of you struggled in this area until I made a decision to allow God to direct me in my relational life. This book will give you insight to that process and also help you to discover a foundation that you can use for your whole life.

I'm writing this book to let you know that God can and will tell you who your mate is! I know, I hear you saying, "Out of all the millions of people, He's got a choice for me? How can that be?" Well, hopefully in these pages I can show you how it happened for me, which will increase your faith. God wants you to have a loving relationship. One of trust, honor, companionship and teamwork, all that you desire!

A DIFFERENT START THIS TIME

"Prayer For God's Help"

I'm not assuming that you're born again or that you even know what that means. I'm also not assuming that you have ever prayed to God before in your life. To tell you the truth, I was well into my life before I realized that I had never really prayed a real prayer. But remember, we're making a decision to do this whole thing related to relationship differently, so I'd like to take you through a little order. If you're able, I need for you to trust me on what I'm about to share.

The first point I'd like for you to trust me on is this: *You need God to help you with this process.* That point should be easy for you. However, you need to trust me on this point as well: *You need Him to help you everywhere in your life.* The one thing many people don't understand about God is that He never comes into a person's life without being invited. This point alone can explain why many people struggle in areas of their lives and God does not get involved because they simple don't invite Him to get involved. You want to be the best you can be, and if you've never considered it before, I'd like to encourage you to make a very important decision. I'm doing something in the process of helping you that is a little different. Believe it or not, this meeting we're having is not just about you finding your mate, even if you thought it was. God has been waiting for you to come to Him and establish a relationship way before now. I want you to consider asking Christ to come into your life.

Because He had you on his mind when His Son died for you, because He wants to be close to you and help you with everything, because He loves you. Normally most books close with an invitation to ask Christ to come into your life after all the information has been read and received. I want you to place the real agenda for success on your entire life and not just on having a great relationship. If you're coming to this story and it's only about getting a husband or a wife, I hate to be the bearer of bad news, but it's going to be a waste of your time. I'm not saying that you can't get something from this, but I am saying that God has the responsibility of making this work both for you and for the other person as well. He's not going to set you up with the one that's right for you and you're not right for them.

I think it's critical that you understand that God is not looking at the outer appearance. Don't panic! That does not mean that your mate won't be attractive, but it does mean that the major factor for God is the inside not the outside. The Bible says that, "Man looks at the outer appearance but God looks at the heart." God is not matching bodies; God is matching hearts. So at the beginning of this process, I'd like to lead you into a heart adjustment on the front end to give you the greatest opportunity for success; not for just a relationship, but for your whole life being more successful and fulfilled. I'd like for you to consider this journey as a turning point for your life.

If you go through this book with me, you'll discover that the real foundation for my discovery of Meriam was not just about finding my mate. It was the platform that began this process, true enough, but finding her was the doorway to God helping me to realizing the relationship aspect that I needed to have with Him. I discovered in the early process of this journey an understanding of the difference between relationship and religion. Religion did not lead me to Meriam, relationship did. I guess you can say, "The relationship led me to a relationship." The path that got me to Meriam was through Him. I'll explain in the chapters coming up, but for now, however, let's just begin with the simple request for God to help you.

First, understand that God loves you and wants the very best for you. He wants to have a relationship with you. He's not interested in just being a matchmaker. And, believe it or not, He's not interested at all in a bunch of religious activity under the umbrella of intimacy with Him. He wants to share His life with you, and He wants you to share your life with Him. So let's begin there. The proper order is "from you to Him and thru Him to them." This prayer is simply taking a step from you to Him. Please don't confuse this with anything you see related to the world's image of the church or any religious grandstanding that goes on. Most of these images misrepresent the true nature and character of God. Most of what is publicized about God and the church in media is not a true representation and has an agenda to drive people away from God, not draw people to Him.

With that in mind, just believe that God wants you to share a relationship with Him for love's sake.

PRAYER

"Dear God, I understand that you cared so much for me that you sent Jesus to pay for my freedom, wholeness and a new life. Thank you for that. I would like to ask you to forgive me for my past and thank you for helping me with my future. I invite you

into my heart so we can grow to become one, in Jesus name!" Amen!

All this simply means is that you have asked God to place in you a new, born-again spirit with Him being in charge.

Being born is instant, but growing up is a process. With this prayer, believe that you have just begun the process of growing up and building a relationship that can take your life to another level. Sure, there's more going on in life than just this prayer, but the seed of God's Spirit has been planted in your heart. Find yourself a good church that will teach you the Word and how to walk in a lifestyle of faith, request water baptism based on your decision in Christ, and spend your own personal time in the Word each day.

MY PRAYER FOR YOU:

Father, as {write your name here} begins this journey through these pages, reveal to them the special message that you have planted in them for their sake. I pray that every word you have given me is a divinely inspired message that will open to them the information that you need for them to have. I agree for the success of their lives in your purpose, and I also agree for success in the area of their relational lives, first with you then through you to the God-ordained relationship for them you desire.

In Jesus Name, Amen

Now, let's get going

I think this is about the 6th or 7th time I've started this book over the past 16 or so years, and I'm determined to make this be the last time before print. I'm sure you're asking why it took so long. Well, I guess I could answer in a word, LIFE, but I think it's also been a spiritual fight. For more than 13 years, I've been the Pastor of a church that was planted from scratch by my parent church, Faith Chapel Christian Center and our pastors, Mike D. and Kennetha Moore and family, My wife, Meriam, and I are raising a family of 4 with two boys at home, a daughter who flies all over the world, and our oldest son who works for Mickey Mouse at Disneyworld in Orlando.

I have to say that allowing God to direct me in making the choice of who I married and binding my own preconceived notions about my wife was only a part of how I got here. If you' re interested in getting to the place of having heaven on earth in relationship then, this book will lead you in the right direction. I would encourage you to read the whole book and pay close attention to not only what God said to me but also HOW He spoke to me. I'll be 59 in a few months, and this is the greatest time of my life. It's also the most challenging. It really comes down to whom you allow to be your guide. I chose to allow God to be my guide and trust that His counsel was going to have a better result than anybody or anything.

The truth is, I've had the experience of the Burger King approach. You know, "Have it your way," and my way resulted in a lot of problems – and that's not just relationship problems. If you're reading this book, then it's almost certain that you're looking for a better way. The institution of marriage has been pulled in many directions. I believe the best way to understand the original intent and design for anything is to look at the very first one.

I'm choosing not to get into the discussion or validity of what or who was first in the arena of creation and marriage. The original for me is the Bible. Don't panic, this won't be a religious rant of telling anyone else how wrong they are for not thinking the same as me. I do believe, however, that this will give you the inside view of the very unusual way God worked in my life, which I believe with all my heart is just an example of what He wants to do for you as well. The Bible says that God is no respecter of persons, and what He has done for one of His children, He will do for another. As one of His children, you can claim and believe for God to move in your life. Don't allow the world and past failure to cause you to adjust your dreams or to cause you to lose hope of what you have in your heart. I never gave up, and today is proof that there is a way to reach the dream of a great relationship and a real marriage.

DIVORCE HAPPENS

Okay, so I'm the director of detention at a local school, and for some reason I asked the students about relationships. It was an explosion of comments from both boys and girls. The students range from grades 7-12, but on this day most were high school students. I can't get into all the details of what I heard, but it made me realize just how far off the mark the relationship process is now. Today, reality shows and entertainment, as well as little to no guidance at home, has all but ruined the fundamental foundation for relationships and the overall platform for two people coming together. The fact that relationship problems are where they are with these high school students just confirms the condition of society. Young people will always let you know the truth in where we are in our culture. Exposure to more and more of the world's dysfunction has created a thirst for more dysfunction that has made dysfunction the norm, and as crazy as it sounds, the goal. I'm calling it the quest for reaching a "Dysfunctional Comfort Zone."

Relationships today are no more complex than they were 100 years ago. You still need a combination of the same things you needed before. Trust, security, honesty, personal happiness, and companionship. Oh, and money, among other things that could be mentioned, depending on who's doing the writing.

But there is a common component that has to be there for a great relationship, and that is two people who know who they are. The other thing that I believe you really need is to have both people be really honest about allowing the Spirit of God to develop them, as well as giving Him the lead position to choose whom you will spend the rest of your life with. I know you've heard that before and you don't believe God will pick your mate for you. Well, that's exactly what I said and even taught others as a minister until it happened to me, so just walk with me and I'll show you how God walked me down this road to a place of now almost 20 years of marriage, which seems like only a year or two, except we have two boys growing up way too fast and two more children that are grown and seeking that place in life for themselves that we all desire to have. Regardless of whether we know it or not, we all desire to be in a place of purpose and a place of close relationship with God. We all also desire to have another person to share that space and journey with us in our lives.

I've always believed that God was real, and even though I had no relationship with Him at the time, something in me had respect for that fact. I "did" church and even sang in the choir and played church softball, but that was the extent of my church experience. My early experience of God consisted of one thing and one thing only, going to church. My parents did the right thing by taking us to church. My dad confesses now, however, that he made the mistake of allowing us to choose between Sunday school or church and that he would not have done that today.

Both my mom and my dad have been active in the First Baptist church on 19th street. back in my hometown of Sheffield, Alabama. Like most teens, when I left home I left the church. The only real praying I did was the Lord's Prayer before I went out to play a game in college or the NFL. Oh! And that time our plane made an emergency landing because we had a bomb threat right after takeoff after a loss to the Bengals. I was married one year out of college at 23, and it was over before I was 32. I found myself single again with two children and a load of personal issues I knew had to handle or I was never going to survive, let alone make it to a real marriage or to just to have a real life. I needed help but didn't know where to turn.

It was during this time of trouble and reflection that I realized that I needed to do some evaluation and changing before I could really have a chance at a real relationship. One thing was for sure with me; I knew I wanted to be married. Can I say to you right at this point to really be honest with yourself about what you really desire? God can't give you want if you're not sure you want. I'm encouraging you to decide right here that the purpose for this connection we're making is for you to be in a committed relationship. If you don't know if you really want that as a part of your life, then get on back out there and just bounce around. But for you that know what you want in your future, this is for you.

It was right here, like many of you, that in the middle of a troubled life I tried to move on with the next chapter by having a relationship with another person and just get married again and move on, but I couldn't get over the hump. Another aspect that drove me toward marriage was the fact that I wanted my two older children to believe in marriage. I wanted them to understand that even though I failed at the marriage, there was nothing wrong with marriage itself. My desire for them is that they would learn to trust that the institution of marriage was real and that one day they would get married for themselves. I understood that the best thing I could do for them was to live out the recovery from the first failed attempt at marriage and transition and show them a great marriage.

It was clear that I was broken, and I couldn't fix me. It was one attempt after another with frustrating outcomes at relationships, with all being done the only way I knew how but hoping for a different outcome.

I was so put out about it that I confronted God. I had no previous personal relationship with God. No conversations, no real praise, no worship, no interaction, and now I'm so done with my life and where I am that I've decided to go to the Creator I've heard about but didn't know personally. Frustration had created "desperation." This place of desperation is where we will start this unusual but amazing Journey.

Before the divorce, I reconnected with the old perception of what I knew of a relationship with God, which meant going to church. I found this church in Opelika, Alabama, that was recommended to me by Coach Joe Whitt (a coach with Auburn University at the time) and his family. I started attending and ultimately joined. The one thing it did for me was to give me clarity as to what I was doing and how much I needed to start over with who I was.

I also used this season in my life to spend one-on-one time with my oldest son, BJ. I would take him with me to Sunday school, then he and I would always go between Sunday school and church to a gas station near the interstate to buy candy and just sit. Our daughter Kelsie was just a baby. Looking back now I realized that I was not saved, but like many people, I thought I was. I grew up going to church and even sang in the choir and was baptized at an early age. I know what you're thinking. "If you did all that, why do you say you were not saved?" Because all those things were good activities for me to do as a Christian, but you'll notice I didn't say anything about truly giving my life to Christ. You can do all those things and never really commit to building a personal relationship with God. That's right! You can get baptized but not make an inward firm decision to allow Christ into your heart. I think many people are guilty of this error not so much on purpose but out of ignorance of what true salvation really means. This place in my life is shifting me toward change.

"THE CONFRONTATION"

Now at this place in my life, I found myself divorced and living in Birmingham.. I was doing what I could do to get over the shock of actually having to start over with my life. I waS living in an apartment with no furniture. I came home every day from my job and sat against the wall and went thru my mail. The job that I had just moved into had to have been from God. Each day was a day of trying to figure out what was going on with me, and I knew that it was at a turning point in my life. What I was claiming as a rededication of my life back a few years back at Pine Grove was really the process of just getting right back into the routine of church activity that was all I knew. It did not take me long to realize that I needed more.

The decision to move to Birmingham was based on believing that it was God. I wanted nothing to do with anything that was not directed by Him. I was struggling with being separated from my very young kids and dealing with my life being at what I felt was a bottom. My boss, Jimmy, has ultimately become one of my closest friends today and was part of what I believe God's plan for saving my life. But I'm not sure at the time he knew it, and to be honest, neither did I.

A period of a year or so had gone by, and I was trying to just move on. I had a close friend of our family from Sheffield, Donnie Flint, invite me to her church, and I accepted and First Baptist Fairfield became my home church. I started with Donnie in the women's Sunday school class and never left. During that time, I grew spiritually in a profound way as Pastor Twyman and my Sunday school teacher, Mrs. Nettie Barns, guided me through the process of an encounter with God that would become the day to remember. I continued from time to time to try and build another relationship. Like most of us, we just try and reach out and start another relationship as if that would fix everything, because after all, most of the time we see the problem as someone else's fault, right?

Well, I had gone in and out of dead end attempts at having a new relational life and for the next few years I was searching for answers. I had other problems in my life that needed to be addressed. Over the years, I had created a mess in my personal life. Here's what I knew for sure: I had problems that needed to be resolved within me, but at the same time, I wanted to go on with my life. This is the same thing some of you are doing right now, and it just doesn't work. The start-over in life was more than just a new person in my life, the real start-over with my life was the fact that I needed to be the new person in my life. The only problem with this situation is that it's a lot easier to change things externally than it is to change things internally. My life was about to make a real internal change.

Out of frustration, I did something that would alter the course of my life forever. I confronted God. No, not by praying to ask him to help me, oh no! That would have been the same old thing. I went at God almost to the point of angry confrontation. I was frustrated and decided to go for a walk and get in God's face. As best as I can remember, I had just come to another dead end with what I thought was a relationship that had potential but turned out to be another empty road. Does this sound familiar?

At this place many people do one of three things. 1. Just settle for anyone and deal with the problems that come along with something not even close to the real vision you may have in your heart, or 2. Just keep going from one person to another and give up on the whole idea of having a real, honest to goodness love story. Then, there's 3. Go to God and find out what He has to say.

Frustration had set in, and I was desperate. In my mind I said, "That's it! I'm done with this mess and I want some answers. If God is who he says he is and If God is real I want him to help me!" So I went outside as if I needed to be clear of buildings and nothing was in the way and this is what I said.

"God, I don't understand why I'm struggling with this relationship thing. Why can't I have a loving relationship! I see young people with them, older people with them and people my age with them. I'm a nice guy and I don't go out of my way to hurt anyone! You say you know everything! So, why can't I have a good relationship? What's wrong with me?" And that's when my life changed forever because I heard these words and it was coming from a direction I had never really recognized before,

"UNTIL YOU LEARN TO LOVE ME, YOU'LL NEVER KNOW HOW TO LOVE ANYONE ELSE."

I knew in an instant that I had just heard a voice that I had not heard before. At least coming from that direction. I heard it from inside and not with my natural ears, but it was clear and distinct. Honestly, my first reaction was, "Who was that?" Walking down the sidewalk, I froze in my tracks. Learning how to love Him implied that there was more than one person involved as the subject of instruction. I realized that God had spoken to me and the encounter showed me several things in this moment of time. (1) God was with me, (2) He understood what I was going thru. (3) He heard me in my desire to reach out to him and (4) He has always been there for me.

Now we all have the basic knowledge of God being the all-knowing Creator of the universe and Maker of all things, but to realize that this same God is able to and desires to come down to our personal level was an eye-opening experience. Ok, I'm a Christian, right? So I have his question: Why was this event such a shock to me? It took me a while before it came to me as to why this was such a moving experience. Before this happened, my relationship with God was like most of ours. The relationship was surrounding services and religious activity. Even in what we consider to be personal relationship we have been trained to connect with God in a religious way. We all are influenced to experience God in different ways depending on how you grew up or where you're from.

However, more than anything else our connection to God is based mainly on a feeling. If you're not saved, then you do whatever you think you need to do to fix the problem of losing in the relationship game. You try changing your look, you try going to web sites, you try blind dates, you try changing the places you go and the people you hang with, but none of that works. For me in this instant I traveled from religion to relationship because I decided to be real with God and just charge into His presence demanding an answer to my problem. I cut through all the form and fashion and just got into God's personal space. I needed help and I knew the only one that could help me was God with this area of my life.

Like everyone, I had other challenges that were life-long challenges that I'm still working on every day. I know your question at this point is, "What does this have to do with finding my mate?" Well, for me (and I believe for you) it was everything! I believe I'm speaking to many of you who are in that same place of frustration but didn't know where to turn for help. Why was this my lightbulb moment and why is this your lightbulb moment? Because now this journey to my mate has taken an unusual turn that I didn't expect or I could say I didn't understand was important. My success in the area of relationships is traveling thru my relationship with God. As I stated earlier, the proper order is "from me to Him to them." What I'm saying to anyone reading this book is that your relationship God has for you is directly connected to your relationship with Him.

Meriam said that at one point early on between us she went to God and asked Him, "Why is Byron not spending more time with me?" She stated that He came right back to her and asked, "How much time are you spending with me?" The point of this issue establishes the proper order.

Here's the greatest benefit to this new understanding that goes well beyond the connection. I now view my wife as an extension of my relationship with God. It is because of Him that it exists. I see her as a gift from Him, so my honor for Him is connected to how I treat her. There are some things I wouldn't do in this relationship, not just because I love my wife but also because I love the God that gave me my wife. Can you see now why so many relationships fall short of the goal of being real and having that extra something to stay together? The extra something is God, not each other alone. A three-fold cord is not easily broken. Little did I know that this one adjustment in my order of life would be the beginning of a walk with

God for more than just finding and living in a better relationship with my future wife, it was the beginning of a new life. Many people struggle in the relationship area because they are out of order and really it's about them and a mate. In a word the truth is that "God is not in it."

Learning how to love God is another experience that takes time and created in me another aspect of a true walk with God. I never really experienced the relationship in a real way until our relationship became real. The distance between religion and relationship with God is about a thousand miles once you understand that there is a difference. Until you realize that there's a difference you don't even know that the road to the other exists. Each day I would ask myself, "How do I learn to love God?" Just the phrase alone means process. I'm now a licensed minister. Appointed to the board of trustees at Auburn University by the governor of the state. I've been hired as the color analyst for Auburn men's basketball and attending Faith Chapel Christian Center. I've gotten the Word from God. You're ready! In my morning reading time the scripture from Proverbs.

I began to do and search for what made sense to me, without success. I've met my now wife, but have not realized that she's my wife and I'm coming up to dead ends again and again in my pursuit of just who it was. Isn't it interesting that you could actually already know your husband or wife and not even be aware of it? I was using all of my common sense and my knowledge and all of my natural perceptions as to the answer to this all-important question for my life and still didn't know that it was her. Maybe you're doing the same thing.

"THE ENCOUNTER"

How we met

The first question you may ask is, "Were you dating?" The answer to the question is "yes," but I think I need to explain. I was not wasting time. At this point in my life I had no need for playing games or going from one place to another to feel as if I was God's gift to women. I was on a mission of getting my life back into order and house and home were part of that. I had what I now know as the guidelines for finding my wife but remember none of the process was a part of this story for me in the beginning.

I didn't get this until the later part of our dating. Every morning my day started the same, reading a chapter of the book of Proverbs. I was ministering by invitation at different churches by this time and had finally gone public with the fact that I was called into ministry at my then church of First Baptist in Fairfield. That's a long story but it was there that I really discovered a personal relationship with the Lord and it grew. I was trying to do relationship the only way I knew how which was dating in a worldly way, but it just wasn't working. Somehow, I knew from this point in my life that I had to have someone in my life who was about ministry and had a real relationship with God and not religious view about God. It was here that the natural thought would be to date someone in church. Well, that's true to a point but not even this was working. Why? Just because a person is going to church does not mean that they have a personal relationship with God. People go to church for all kinds of reasons, just like people don't go for all kinds of reasons. I didn't know much about the person I would eventually be with, but I did know that they had to be serious about their walk with God. Listen, I had gone through the stages of anger about my divorce saying stuff like "I'll never let another woman into my life that close again." Then after a few years of that mindset the truth about my desire to have a family with and near me was much stronger than the anger that I had felt.

One day at my job I received a phone call from a woman who wanted me to come and minister at her church for a singles conference. She said that she had heard about me and wanted to know if I would come and share. I realize now as I think about it that my message was about the subject of following God and not as much about being single at all. Just before I was to speak I would always find a quiet place to pray so I asked someone if there was a place I could go and be alone. They pointed me downstairs. So I went to the basement of the church to pray. There was a guy already down there. We spoke, and I soon realized that guy was who is now my brother-in-law, Travis Spencer. While I walked around praying, I kept hearing another voice coming from a dark side of the room, but I didn't see anyone. I asked Travis, "Hey! Where is that voice coming from?" He said, "Oh, that's my sister on the phone in the other area in the dark." I don't think she came out before I left, but that was Meriam. It wasn't until after both Travis and I finished that I realized that her entire family was there to hear Travis. It is amazing that God introduced me to my new family that day all at the same time. Did I know it? No.

You see, I had my mind on ministry and not on anything else. God was putting us together the entire time, but I didn't know it. There were many things that I had to deal with in my life yet to come but the introduction had been made. How crazy is it that you could actually encounter God's plan for your life and you not even be aware of it? Just knowing this will make you think a little more about who is around you.

I think the key to this point is that I was busy doing what I had been called to do with kingdom business. I was on the path. "What path" you may ask. There is a path that God set for your life and you can choose to walk in it or you can choose to walk on your own path. On his path are people, places and things He desires for you to encounter. On your path are people places and things God does not desire you to experience. This is why it is so much better to do things God's way and not your own. After the service I met everyone, and Naomi introduced me to her parents and her sister Meriam. She was a tall, attractive woman with braces and was very quiet. Did I think this was my wife? No. I had a young lady from the church I was attending to actually invite herself to go with me, so at the time I actually had someone with me, but we were not dating. A few weeks later, Naomi called and asked if she could come by and bring a gift for me speaking and I said yes. When she came by, she thanked me for speaking and said that it went very well and I did exactly what she wanted for that service.

Then she said this: " You should ask my sister out because she is an awesome woman of God, and she is the greatest person I know." I told her that I wasn't really trying to get into a relationship right now but thanks. She said, "Okay, but I really think you should." A few more weeks went by, and she called me again. She said that she and her then fiancé were going out and wanted to know if I would come and go with Meriam as well. My first thought was the last thing I want to do is to sit somewhere with 3 people I didn't know that I didn't want to be with, so I said, "I tell you what, I'll call her and ask her to lunch." In my mind I was thinking, "I'll get it over with so she will leave me alone about her sister." She kept saying that she was the most awesome woman she knew. I told her, "It's your sister, what else would you say?" I had people try and set me up before, and I ran from most based on the people that were doing the setting up. In this case, at least this was a woman with an entire family that was interested in supporting one another and seemed to be kingdom-minded.

Anyway, I didn't know it, but my life was about to change forever.

I had decided that I was going to be myself. I had nothing to lose, and I was going to show this girl who I am now. I was all about who God had made me to be, and I wasn't putting on for anybody. If they didn't like it, I didn't care. I was determined to be myself with this woman and just talk Jesus to this girl and see run her away from my life. Boy, did that backfire!!! So I called her and told her who I was and asked if she would like to go to lunch and she said "Yes."

So I went by to pick her up. I went inside to get her, and she looked really nice. I open the door for her and she gets in the car and I got my gospel music playing and asked if she had any idea where she wanted to go. It's funny because the last person that I went out with said to me, "That's enough of that gospel music." She didn't know it, but that was my cue to get going.

I really can't tell you much after that but the only things I remembered about that lunch was this. First, it was the most different feeling I had ever had in that I was totally myself and it was okay. This girl was different. She was not like anyone I had gone out with. She was real. I noticed her because her comments to me were unlike anything I'd ever heard before. As I talked to her about God and the church she said, "You're going to do great things for God."

I talked and talked and talked and she sat and listened, listened and listened. When I dropped that girl off I said this, "What was that?" I had never been on a lunch like that before and I said that I need to take that girl out again, not to mention she looked really good. Something was different about this woman. Without going through the next few years, I will just say that as we began to go out more I saw all the qualities I knew were the qualities I was wanting and needing in my life. I continued to see other people at times, but it was because I was still trying to fit them into my own mental concept. There was nothing fake about Meriam and I knew that if I allowed myself to, it would get really serious very quickly and I was afraid of that and I didn't know if she was God's choice yet.

I sat down for dinner with a perfect stranger and he said, "Why aren't you married?"

We were somewhere in Spain and I was traveling with the Auburn basketball team as a guest as a member of the board of trustees during my 12 year term. I don't remember his name, but he was the travel promoter and set the entire two week travel tour up for the team. My answer to him was, "I'm expecting to have the answer to that while I'm here." I was confessing that God would help me get the answer to that question, maybe because I would be away from everybody and would be able to hear a little clearer or maybe because there would be very little else to do. Either way, I believed I could get some answers. Then he asked a question that directed me to my wife. The question was, "Are you seeing anyone?" So what was the answer to his question?

I said to him, "There's this one girl, but I don't think she's the one." Don't panic, Meriam has heard this testimony before, and I'll get into the specifics of that later on. He said, "Oh? Tell me about her." So I began talking about her in detail starting with how pretty she was and what a godly women she was and how great she was with my two children and how smart she was and on and on and finally he stopped me and said, "She sounds like the one to me! What's wrong with her?" That's when I heard the Holy Spirit say, "Yeah, what's wrong?" Here's a little heads-up: Anytime God ask you a question, He already knows the answer, but He's just helping you to see it too!

This was not His first time pointing me to Meriam. It was a morning just like the other mornings when I sat up and flipped to Proverbs to get my day started. The Spirit of God said to me, "Go to Exodus," and I said, "Exodus" out loud! Then I said, "You know we always start our day in Proverbs!" So I just flipped in one turn to Exodus and there it was, Ex. 15:20, "And Miriam the prophetess the sister of Aaron took a timbrel in her hand and all the other women went out after her with timbrels and with dances." This was before my trip, so this dinner conversation just confirmed what was already going on.

I began to realize what God was doing, but I was still not convinced. I left that dinner table and felt like I needed to just call and say hello to Meriam and I'm not sure how long I had been gone but gave her a call. I later found out that she did remember me calling and wondering, why is he calling me from Spain? Which tells you that we were not officially dating at the time. Anyway, the trip goes on and comes to an end and we get back to Atlanta and I get into my car and head back to Alabama. I went to see my parents up in Sheffield instead of going straight home. I just wanted to check on them and let them know I was back and okay. So on my way back to Birmingham I turned off my radio and said this prayer: "Lord, I don't know who my mate is, I think you are saying it's Meriam, but I'm still not sure, but if it is, don't let me miss the sign., Amen."

This prayer was as much for her as it was for me. The last thing I wanted to do was to take myself and someone else into a direction that God didn't have planned for their life.

Well, I continued on home and got to my house and was just glad to be home. It was such a nice day that I decided to go outside and take a little walk around our neighborhood and that's when I got hit right between the eyes. I stood in my front yard talking to one of my good friends and as we talked I noticed in every yard was the sign for a city council race going on " Vote for Meriam Witherspoon." Her slogan, "It's time to move forward." Not only was it a sign; it was what was on the sign!!! I was shocked with that one. Even the slogan God had been given to me at my job on the sidewalk in the form of a UNO game card. "Move forward 2." I didn't know it at the time, but the card was a type of sign to move on to the second one. This was years before now but at the time of finding the card I didn't know what the second one was but I had a small idea. Those two signs though years apart were connected to me. I know this is crazy, but it gets better. The singles ministry was meeting down in Destin, Florida, for a group trip, but I had to go thru Auburn for a called board meeting then I was to travel on down to Destin to meet up with the ministry trip.

Leaving Birmingham, I now knew that Meriam is God's choice. My meeting ended, and I had lunch and took off for the singles trip. I got lost on the drive so who do I call? You got it! Meriam. So she gives me directions to lead me to the resort, and I hang up the phone and the Holy Spirit says, "See, she is your helper," "Oh my God!" I said to myself, "Meriam is my wife!"

CHAPTER 1

The First Question

Everyone has a set of questions related to getting into that one relationship they see themselves in. Where should I go to find this person? How will I know them when I see them? What will they be doing and the number one question: Who is it? It's only natural to have this as the main focus of that journey because after all this is the main issue of your getting the relationship under way that you desire to have. Most people just keep seeing people until one sticks. The problem with this process is you end up stuck to folks you have a really hard time getting unstuck from. They end up like gum on your shoe on a hot day. This is an endless process that causes more problems than results.

Here's a plan. Step back for a moment and just work on you. If you're frustrated with the endless cycle of coming back to the same place, then you need to just stop. Sometimes you bring so many trees into the mix that you can't see the forest. Here's another problem, and it's a big one—you don't know what you're looking for. You just think you do. So how do you know? All I can really tell you is that for me it all came down to trusting that God would help me. I didn't know about the first question, but I guess you could say I found it the same way I discovered all of this I'm sharing with you now.

At this point I had been by myself for several years and

each morning began with about 20-30 min. or longer of the book of Proverbs. I moved into a place of really being settled in growing in God and living a life that was focused on being all that I could be based on what was going on with me spiritually. It was my regular process each morning and it happened! On this morning, Proverbs chapter five was in my plan. I had read it before, probably 1000 times, but this time it was personal and directly to me. "Drink waters out of thine own cistern, and running waters out of thine own well. Let them be only thine own and not strangers with thee." The word "Possession" leaped on the inside of me, and I knew God was saying to me, "It's time, you're ready"

I believe that most people do the same thing that I had done in the process of finding that relationship. We search high and low and go from place to place and from failed attempt to failed attempt ending up frustrated and confused about why things are so hard in the relationship area. I'd gone thru some pretty challenging struggles getting to that morning but at the end of the day I heard from God about timing. As much as we would like to think we're ready for that next step to have a relationship the truth is most of us are not. I had been given most of this process for the book in finding and choosing and thought to myself after seeing it unfold that this is going to be a great lesson to teach the singles. Not realizing that God was actually working on me in my personal life. After hearing this word from God I realized that the first question in the quest toward a relationship that will really work was not, "Who are they?" The first question for each of you as a single person is simply this: "Am I ready?" So now it's God's endorsement of timing that becomes the right question to be answered.

Here's your challenge: you can't answer that question! Only

God can!

If you answer it, you'll say, "Yes!" Most of the time it would be your flesh speaking loud and clear. Taking you into a tail-spin of problems. A small amount of the time you may be right about being ready, but it will still be a mistake without the direction of the Spirit of God.

So, as for me, I knew I had God's endorsement to move toward having my own. Then, I ran right out and messed up again and got ahead of God. You see, I found out that just because He says its time doesn't mean you can now go out and do whatever you want to in picking. He said to me that it was time, not now you can go and do the rest on your own. Remember, you don't know what you're looking for so how can you pick what you don't know?

You must be willing to let God do his work on you in your own life before you can begin to enter into a real loving God type of relationship. None of us really want to admit it but we're all a work in progress and really need that time alone with God to get to who we really are and shave away our past, our hurts, our fears and our trash. If you're going to have a real shot at love, you're going to have to go back and admit your role in the past problems and shed the issues and "travel light" Your next shot will stand more of a chance. That process for me is a book within itself and a lot of the years leading into the events of this morning I'll discuss a little more but I there were days of feeling sorry for myself, being upset, but waiting on God. I said this and I meant it, "I'm not getting married again until I hear God in this ear and the other one." Well, that was the perfect place to wait on God, and I was really willing to wait. And hear this, I had even decided that if God wanted me to just stay by myself, I was willing to do just that.

Ask the right first question and be willing to hear God say to you, "It's time for you to possess your own." Proverbs 24:27 says that we should "prepare ourselves without"—without what? In this situation you should prepare yourself without a relationship. The rest of that text says to "make it fit for thyself in the field." This means that you need to make the things in your life fit for you first before you add someone else into your life. Then it says "afterwards build thine house." We're trying to build our life with another person before we have made things fit in our own lives. If your life doesn't fit for you, how is someone else going to fit in it? With God's help on the front end you can begin with the right foundation that will really give you a chance to experience the kind of relationship that you have searched for all your life. Ask the right question first: Am I ready?

"You can never learn to stand side by side with another person until you learn to stand on your own." That means you have learned to really be a full person on your own and really be a single who is winning in life. It's taken me years to really realize that even now I'm still learning to stand on my own two feet and that's even in marriage! It's critical for you, in your relationship, that you have an independent understanding of who you are, what you can do and where you're going. Here's why:

There could be a time even in your relationship that not even your spouse will be able to see, understand or maybe even believe that what you see and believe is something you are capable of or called to do. In that situation you have to believe in yourself and decide to stay with it, even if you have to stand by yourself. It does not mean your relationship is not good, it just means that your spouse can't see what you see. That happens even in great relationships. You could be wrong but some things you have to come to an end to on your own, even if you're the only one walking it out. That can only happen when you are settled in who you are. Winning as a single means that you are in control of your flesh because if you're chasing women or men now as single, a marriage license won't change that. It means having your finances in order and not being covered up in bills as a single person. If you can't pay your bills as a single, you certainly can't do it with a partner. How about your body? If you're in bad shape now, you can bet it's not going to get better. Your relationship will not be able to have quality longevity if you're in poor health.

CHAPTER 2

"Until You Learn To Love Me, You'll Never know how to Love Anyone Else"

I had great example at home growing up. No fussing, no arguing. Just teamwork. The only time I ever saw any disagreement at all was when it was time to go to events and my mom wanted to stay at home; she was a homebody! So, I didn't get wrong relationship advice from them. Maybe it came from the Ohio Players, The O'Jays or some of my musical influences during that time or like many of us, from the streets. Somehow, I believe the pressure of the environment shaped my view of just what relationship and dating was all about. I realize now that I didn't know how to have a true healthy relationship with anyone because I didn't have one with God. How did I come to this great revelation and what does a relationship with God have to do with dating or even marriage? Well, this is what I discovered…

It was a nice summer day, and I was walking down the sidewalk disgusted about another failed attempt at relationship. I'd been divorced two to three years at that time, and I was stuck. I wanted to move past my past, but I couldn't. With the pain, hurt and fear holding me back I couldn't move on. Much of the time it was the ongoing issues in the current aspect of my life that made the idea of committing to another relationship so difficult yet still I had had enough! My past was in my present life and I couldn't move forward.

So, I'm on this walk fussing at God, like it was His fault. Now, remember up to this point I had no real relationship with God. I did church and even did church activity, but I've discovered that this was the first real conversation I directed to God in a real way. So this is how it went. "God, I don't understand this, I see younger folks, older folks and folks my age happy in relationships, so I know it's possible and you say you know everything, so why am I having such a hard time? You say you know everything! I'm a nice guy and I don't go out of my way to hurt anybody so what's the problem with me having a real relationship?" Then it happened

That's when I heard these words, "UNTIL YOU LEARN TO LOVE ME, YOU'LL NEVER KNOW HOW TO LOVE ANYONE ELSE!" I froze in my tracks and said these words, "Who was that?!" Deep inside I heard those words, but I quickly realized that they came from a different direction from that of my own thoughts. I knew that I had just heard from God.

It was here on that sidewalk in Hoover, Alabama, that my life changed forever.

I realized in that instant that God was there. He was in my moment, He became real and in an instant, I went from religion to relationship. Maybe you're in religion and not a relationship with God. Oh, don't get me wrong! I went to church, I sang in the choir, but I didn't know God or even love Him.

I've always heard people say they heard God's voice and I like most of you felt that the person had lost it. I. When you're not in the Word, you will never really hear God's voice because,

1 God speaks with his Word as his reference point. God never talks outside of the framework of his Word. I was angry, and I wanted an answer. That's when my life changed forever. I was walking outside down a sidewalk venting my frustration to the God I knew of but did not know and bang! I heard him deep within me. I knew in a second That God knew everything about me. He knew what I was feeling, and I knew that he knew everything that had ever happened to me.

So, the journey began. With my effort to learn to love Him, I had no idea he was prepping me for the one thing I had been longing for, real relationship that was my true heart's desire. The first step to the goal will always begin with you and God.

Here are some major points on His statement:

1. The major issue with relationships is that we can try to love someone and not even know love itself because Love is a person not a feeling. At best we show a surface, human type of love and God was saying to me that until I entered a love relationship with him and get to know Him as Love I wouldn't know how to love anyone else, not even myself.
2. God is love, and when we attempt relationship without being taught how to love by love, it will always fall short and end in disappoint.
3. You will only be able to love others to the level that you are willing to love Him.

The Bible asks the question, "How can you say you love a God that you cannot see and you don't love your brother you can see?" Notice that the two relationships are connected. God sees the love you have for Him by how you love others, but I submit to you that you can see the love that you have for others by how much you love God.

Ultimately, if you hold back in your relationship with God, you'll hold back on your relationship with another person.

So right here is a good time to evaluate your love relationship with God and oh, by the way, you can use this as a prime tool for measuring your potential mate. This is a great place to start because if they don't have this one right the rest will be shaky at best.

What does that love of God look like?

It carries a real heart for a relationship with Him. That's more than just going to church. It is a desire to really get to know Him and a real desire to please God.

You can always continue to do the same thing in your attempt to reach your relationship goal but as a close friend of mine use to say, "If you always do what you've always done you'll always get what you've always gotten," it may be time to do something a little different. I realized that my way was not working and in fact had brought me to this place of frustration and unsatisfied relational life. I made the decision of getting to know God because I wanted a second shot at a real relationship and marriage and I knew that it would only happen through a relationship with God Himself.

"LIFE'S GREATEST FIGHT"

The Fight Between You and Yourself

Ok, we've decided to go a step further into the process and get it right based on God's direction instead of the same old thing. Before you can take the next steps of getting to the place of a better relationship there's another important activity you need to engage and that's the fight. The fight of protecting the "You" that needs to be alone from the "you" that wants to be with someone!

We all have several different sides to ourselves. In the process of getting back to having a good relationship you will have a fight on your hands. Most people men in general always fix relationships with relationships or I guess both men and women can be accused of this. The worst thing you could do in the process of starting again is to not deal with yourself. The truth is it took two people to mess up the last relationship, and you better figure out what your role was, or it could and probably will happen again. At the very least you need to know why you chose that person. That decision was your fault, remember? The real "You" never goes down without a fight. The habits, mind sets and way of doing things that has been built up over many years are a part of everything you've done. Now it's time to go in a different direction but the old you will not go quietly into the night. Change is a tough thing to do unless one thing is in place, "desperation" You have to be desperate to go on before you can go.

Now that I've realized I needed to do things differently I was smart enough to know I would have a real fight on my hands. You can call it flesh if you're spiritual or you can call it pre-programmed thinking but here's the point: You must protect the you who needs to learn to stand alone from the you that wants companionship. I know you're saying to yourself " I'm not trying to be alone, that's true but here's the next statement, " you can never learn to stand side by side with another person until you have learned to stand on your own."

So, I picked a fight with myself and began to align my thoughts and efforts with God's foundations for life and every time my own ideas tried to force its way into control I would punch them right back down. It was a fight to the death and I was determined that the man following God was going to win. Listen, this is a fight to the finish not a fight to co-exist! Many times, we try and co-exist with our old life, and that's just not possible.

This is not just true for relationships. I discovered that as it relates to your personal health, especially when it comes to substance abuse. If you've ever been in a fight related to addiction you know that that guy must die in order for the real you to live. Well, it's a fight with the addiction of doing things by your own flesh and not by God's standards.

The most challenging thing to come to grips with after having failed in relationships is the fact that you are the main problem. The same guys or women keep coming because the same person keeps picking. I'm not going to go into the choosing or finding process as much as I want to talk about the person doing the finding and choosing. I knew this about my future. I would never have a great relationship if I didn't get honest with myself about me. I knew I could not have a good relationship If I didn't really figure out how I got into the mess I got into the first time. Guess what? That is not even about the last persons problems and issues or even the person before that! That bit of information is about the you that was before all of that.

Once upon a time there was this little boy who use to ride his bike to Sander's store in our community for the sole purpose of buying three Snickers bars—one to eat right then, one for when he got home, and one for later. This little guy had no hang-ups, no fears and really had none of the issues that had been accumulated over time. Why is this important? Because I decided that whatever it took for me to do I was going to do everything I could to get back to that little boy. Not the candy part but the freedom part.

Too many of us are trying to go on with our lives after having added too much baggage to our life and we take all that junk from one place to another like we do when we move from house to house, sooner or later you have to just throw some stuff away or you turn your new house into the place you left from but its located in a different place. Guess what? It's time to throw some stuff away in your life and get back to the original little care-free, worry-free spirit you were before. That's what salvation does for those who embrace it. Old things pass away behold all things become knew or maybe we can say they become renew.

However, the fight comes when that you that wants somebody right now says, "I want somebody now," but the you that wants to get relationship right for the long term has to be the one of reason and say, "No, lets unload all this junk first and give us the best chance to have what we really want." And the fight is on. Honesty is the key component for you in this place of having this personal battle. If you're a drunk you have to deal with that. If you have a drug problem you have to deal with that. If you are a spending nut you have to deal with that. If you can't keep your pants up you have to deal with that. I can go on and on, but this is the place of digging into yourself that is somewhat working on your past but not from the standpoint of choosing or finding the other person as much as it is on not dumping trash on them when you do. This is the preliminary work that has to be done to lay the groundwork for a plan of success. As you can tell the process of fighting yourself is a combination of self- evaluation which deals with the dark places in your life as well as helps you to build a spiritual foundation of you walk with God.

CHAPTER 3
PLAYER 101

"I give them the dream"

Now those so-called players won't like this very well and every woman should stand up and clap for this bit of info. I'm not sure if any men fall for this trick but this will mess up some of the game for those who like to travel from one person to another.

I knew a guy who always seemed to get women and I asked him once, "Man, how do you keep getting these women?" His answer to me was in a single statement, "I give them the dream." I had no idea what that was, so I asked him what does that mean. And he said, "I make them believe that I'm the one that will make all their dreams come true!" I said ok, like what?

"Well, you listen to them talk and tell you all the things that they are believing for and looking for and searching for and just begin to play that role or place those same things in your conversation as the same things."

That's pretty rough! But it's important for you all to understand that there are actually men and women who play that type of game just to get what they really want. So, how can you protect yourself from such a deceptive attack you may ask because everyone has dreams for their lives. How can you defend yourself against that? It's easy. There are two very important steps to the area of choosing though we aren't there yet.

(1) Some things are better kept between you and God. It's called the compatibility test. Let him share what his goals are. Sometimes you have to not do all the talking. Tell God the answers you want to hear and see if he spends the right amount of time with God. God will give him the answers to the test you're looking for.

(2) No sex! the act of having sex was created by God and it was created for two people in marriage to share the ultimate experience of intimacy. You can't get any closer than that. This level of intimacy needs to be the last level of sharing of yourself after they have committed to you the decision to journey the rest of the way in this life with you. It's a fact that you will get answers about what a person really wants when sex is not clouding the issue.

In today's worldly attitude and position this kind of thinking is considered out of date, but remember, I'm just giving you another option. Don't give them what you have until they give you the dream. That's right! Your only protection from the player 101 is for you to hold on to the one thing that matters most which is "YOU." Ladies, the main agenda for a guy like this is to get you to start assuming the role of a wife while you're still single. Single is single and married is married. His goal is for you to satisfy his needs for free. Then maybe pay you later.

I read another article on that great information source of Facebook that said there is no such thing as a diamond scarcity. In fact, there are millions of diamonds locked away in a vault in London to create the image of diamonds being very rare and expensive. The slogan "diamonds are forever" was created to make them seem valuable, and then they withheld the availability to create the rise in market value.

I'm not 100% sure but I believe the same is done with oil, although the demand for oil is a little different than the market for diamonds. So, the whole point of withholding the diamonds giving them more value is an interesting point. I guess it's easy to understand that when something is in abundance, it loses its ability to be valuable but when it's not easily obtained it become more valuable. I'm not a psychologist, but some of this makes a little since when talking about the issue we are discussing with getting into good relationships. The question that has to be dealt with is this: Does he want you, or does he want what you have? Well, the only way to find that out is to only give him you and hold on to what you have until he buys you. I know that sounds old and out of date, but if you don't want to be fooled by another dream buster, you have to do what it takes to find out the real answer.

Is it me that he or she really wants? Since we're talking about diamonds, I'll share what is my attempt at a parable.

"THE PARABLE OF THE RING"

A man had a very expensive Jewelry store and in it was a very rare diamond ring. A customer came in and showed great interest in the rare stone. So the owner gave the customer a great but unusual option.

"Why don't you take this stone in this ring and wear it for about six to eight months then come back and buy it later?" The owner was really excited because with the purchase of this stone he would be able to retire from his job and go away for his dream life. The customer was very excited about that as an option as well because you couldn't just go anywhere to have that option but because this store was willing to give it to him up front he jumped at the chance.

So the customer went out saying great things to the owner while going out to enjoy this very special ring. The eight months went by, and the owner of the store began to worry but in came the customer. With great excitement, the owner said to the customer, "I'm so excited to see you because I've been looking forward to you coming back to buy the ring you were so excited about." But now there was a problem with the customer. The store owner could tell something had changed with the customer's attitude.

There was no excitement in his voice, and he began to say that he had been thinking that maybe this was a little too expensive for his budget. He was saying that although it looked good, he discovered another ring that was a little less expensive that would look just as good and he wanted to maybe see if he could try it for a while to decide about buying it. Well, the store owner was hurt and angry because the customer promised to buy the ring. Now instead of having a ring that was brand new, everyone around town knew that it was used. The customer went everywhere showing the ring around and telling everyone how he was wearing it to try it out. After the customer left, more and more customers came into store, but now they all wanted the same deal. They didn't want to buy the ring, they only wanted to wear it for a while and give it back. They felt that now that it had been worn they should have to pay less for it.

You are the ring that's behind the counter. The purchase for you is the wedding! Sex before marriage is setting you up to be hurt and disappointed. It also puts the ability to get to know who the person is on hold because the physical aspect becomes more of a priority than the relational growth. The purchase is the dream not the promise of the purchase. Don't allow yourself to be played on a promise and hold on to your most valuable possession until they seal the deal. If they decide to move on you have your answer and you have chosen well which will save you the trouble of the pain and anger that comes with the game.

CHAPTER 4
CLOSE YOUR EYES AND SEE WITH YOUR SPIRIT

"Seeing with the Right Set of Eyes"

This is a tough one! Not because it's hard to do but because it's using eyes most people never use much if at all. You know what happens when you use muscles for the first time? First of all, it's uncomfortable. The other thing is, you don't use them very well. Today we are so overloaded by the media that pushes relationship at us from a natural perspective. All these reality shows are giving a worldly approach to life in relationship that is all wrong. "Close your eyes and see with your spirit" sounds super spiritual and gives you the impression of doing something that my pastor calls goofed up stuff.

He say's "Some stuff we do in the body of Christ is just goofy that it scares people away from God, so He says, 'Don't do goofy stuff!'"

But seeing with your spirit is not as strange as it sounds and it's not as difficult as one might think. Before I give my personal account of this discovery, I'd like to give a biblical explanation to the fact that you have another set of eyes. Ephesians 1:18 says, "The eyes of your understanding being enlightened; that you may know the hope of his calling, and what the riches of the glory of his inheritance in the saints." So this shows that there is another set of eyes beyond your physical eyes. These eyes give you understanding, which means you can be looking with your natural eyes but lack understanding of what's there. Doesn't that explain a lot of the relationship problems we are seeing. So many of the issues we encounter within relationships are based on the fact that we're using our natural eyes to make decisions regarding others we are attempting to have that next level relationship with, but we lack total understanding as to who these people really are.

In 2 Kings 6:17, Elisha prayed that the eyes of his servant would be opened who was afraid because they were surrounded by the enemy. The Lord did, and the Bible said he saw the mountains full of horses and chariots of fire round about them. If you can see things that are there that are working for, you can also see things that are working against you but only with the other set of eyes. You are at a disadvantage if all you are doing is going by your natural eyes only. I told you this would be a tough one because many of us have never used these spiritual eyes before and like the scripture says, you lack understanding with out them. You can use your eyes and don't see a thing! Boy does that sound familiar? It's only after we have gone through the hardship of that failed relationship that we see who that person truly was along with the headache, pain and disappointment. Do you always see everything? No, but you trust God for what you cannot see because you followed the spirit on what he showed you in the spirit. I know it sounds really spiritual but I will show you that it's really not as spiritual as it sounds.

How did I come to this bit of info you ask? I had come back from Spain. I was traveling at the time with the Auburn basketball team as the color commentator. I had been back to Birmingham for maybe a day and was meeting up with the singles group down in Florida for a singles trip that was put on by our singles ministry at Faith Chapel. Before getting with the singles I had to make a stop in Auburn for a Board meeting. Several things happened on that trip to Spain that pointed me to Meriam as my wife, and by this time I had come to the realization that it was really her that God was saying was my wife. Remember at this time I'm like most people who didn't think God would get that detailed with you on such a decision.

My issue with Meriam was that in my mind I was thinking that the person would already have kids (and she didn't), or that the person didn't want to have children, or it was someone my age or closer to my age than Meriam is. In other words from the picture in my mind she was not fitting what I thought. Remember, I even got lost on the drive and called Meriam who guided me to the boat where they were and at that moment, as I said earlier, the Lord said to me "See, that's your helper."

Yet still I was struggling with the notion of that idea even though in my heart I knew what God was saying and for the entire trip down to Florida I went thru the situation in my mind. By the time I got there, however, I knew it was 100% true. I'm a little cloudy on when things happened but I'm not cloudy at all on the event. Just like I always I woke up to grabbing my Bible and turning to Proverbs chapter for the day. Just to remind you of the account this is what happened. I heard the voice of the Lord say, "Go to Exodus" My first thought and comment was, "Exodus! God you know we always read Proverbs in the morning", as if I was calling the shots. Anyway, I literally reached to the front of the Bible and flipped the pages straight to Exodus. Let's not even consider the odds of doing that, but without knowing where I was going or what chapter, I looked down and there it was:

> Exodus 15:20 "And Miriam the prophetess, the sister of Aaron, took a timbrel in her hand; and all the women went out after her with timbrels and with dance."

I sat there for a moment in shock because remember, in my mind at the time, God does not tell you who to marry. I knew what God was saying to me. I received it in my spirit, but my mind was struggling. I tried to dismiss it as just a coincidence, but it was too far to reach for that. God was saying all the other women are behind her. She is the leader. I think for a while I just put it in the back of my mind to say it didn't happen or that it was just some random experience but in my spirit I knew. As I reflect on this event I'm remembering timelines a little more and this happened before I left to go to Spain.

I got to Auburn and made it in time to walk into the meeting and speak to all of our board members and associates. It was a half a day called meeting, so I was on my way before noon. I grabbed lunch at the hotel and made my way toward Florida. Remember, I got lost on the way and God confirmed that Meriam was my helper because I called her to help me find the place.

I met the group on a boat as we prepared to take a short cruise around the harbor and at that moment, driving to the harbor, I knew she was the one. I said to myself, "When I see her, I'm going right over to her and tell her what I've discovered."

Well, I found a park, ran up the plank to board the boat and greeted some of my friends. At the same time, I was looking for

Meriam. Finally, after a few moments of greeting friends and small talk, I saw her; however, instead of running over to her in excitement like I had planned to do, I froze in my tracks and just stood there. I had it all planned out in my head, but when it was time to do it I just froze. For several minutes I just stared at this woman that now I realized is to be my wife.

It was sort of the feeling I had when I was sitting in my parent's bedroom alone watching the NFL draft back in 1981. I had to be alone because it was just too much to deal with being around a bunch of people. The first round was gone, and the second round was well into process. Then it happened, Pete Rozelle stepped up to the podium and said, "With the 22nd pick in the second round, the Buffalo Bills select Byron Franklin, wide receiver, Auburn University." At that moment I just froze. I heard my parents scream in the front of the house and then the phone rings and it's the Bills and then the media.

This event is the closest thing that I can use to even come close to that moment on this boat. All of my years of working out, all of my sacrifices and all of my dreams of reaching that day had happened. In the same way, all of my praying and all of that waiting to get myself together and all of that work on myself preparing for the time when I would go on the journey with the one He would connect with me and all those conversations with God about my life had come to the place when I would try marriage again. The moment had come to this one point in time, and I was in an emotional place I had never been before. I just froze. I saw her, but I couldn't move.

In that second, out of nowhere a very close friend walks up to me and says, "Are you struggling with something God has told you to do?" Shocked by the random question, and also shocked by the fact that it was what was going on, I had no other answer but, "Yes." Without telling me what the question was about, she just walked off. I found out later she was watching me from across the other side of the boat and said that I had the strangest look on my face standing in one spot looking like, as she put it, someone had just stolen my Big Wheel and so she asked God, "Lord what is wrong with Byron?" And she said He responded right back to her saying 'He's struggling with something I've told him to do."

She came right over to me and asked if that was what was going on. Well, I did finally go over to Meriam and we did chat, but I did not say a thing about what had been going on. Is that crazy or what? We both went about doing all the activities and functions and would chat and go about the vacation as a group. There was jet skiing, hang gliding and all sorts of things to do and most of the time it was the guys together and ladies hanging in groups as well. I spent the entire weekend on that singles trip dealing with the realization of what I had discovered while trying to enjoy a group vacation. I still didn't say anything. One night I just went out to the beach as the sun was setting and thought about what was going on and was still trying to catch my mental emotional and spiritual breath.

It's Saturday now and I've asked my pastor if he had a moment that we could talk. He is always willing to take time with all of his members to spend a few moments even with it being thousands of them and he said, "Sure." We decided to go out on the main street area and walk on the sidewalk. Let me say that I did not tell him everything I had gotten because I didn't want him to think I was spiritually goofy and put out a bunch of signs myself for my wife, but I did tell him that I believed God was saying to me that it was Meriam. While walking with him and just kind of pouring out my heart to him on the matter I got advice on what I was dealing with. So with love and fatherly guidance he gave me counsel and we talked. With wisdom he leaves the ultimate decision right where it began, with me, but he had great things to say about Meriam.

I do remember, however, that my main point to him was that it didn't look like I thought related to who the person would be. I didn't get to how I felt about Meriam but the truth was I knew that I was in love with her very early on, but with him I only wanted to deal with the spiritual aspect of the situation. We walked a bit longer then turned around and went back. Just before the trip was to end we had a church service in a little meeting room with everyone on the trip to sort of end the vacation as a group and during the service, out of the blue, a member of the group stands up and says, "I have a word from the Lord!" I'm sitting in the back of the room not really paying attention to the full moment but still taking everything in; then the words that closed this entire weekend and my perspective on the matter came out. This was it, the next moments that would change my life again, forever. At this point I still hadn't said anything to Meriam. I had at least 4 or 5 of these moments with God speaking to me making it clear to me who He had found for me and I guess you could say this was the closing argument. Sarah Verser then walks up to the front of the room and says, "I have a word," so she walks to the front and says:

> Isaiah 11:1-3 said, "And there shall come forth a rod out of the stem of Jesse, and a Branch shall grow out of his roots. And the spirit of the lord shall rest upon him, the spirit of wisdom and understanding, the spirit of counsel and might, the spirit of knowledge and of the fear of the lord. And shall make him of quick under-

standing in the fear of the Lord". She said, "AND HE SHALL NOT JUDGE AFTER THE SIGHT OF HIS EYES, NEITHER REPROVE AFTER THE HEARING OF HIS EARS."

BOOM!

The last part of that scripture blew up in me and was like a punch to my belly. Also, to add to the moment, the pastor got up from his seat in the very front of the room and walked to the back of the room where I sat, pointed at me and said, "Did you get that word?" He then turned and walked back to his seat. So not only did I hear the word that was spoken directly to me, but the man I have great respect for and see as my teacher and spiritual father figure heard the exact same thing.

What was God saying to me this time? He was teaching me a very important step in the process of discovering the person God has for me and I'm giving it to you now as well. What I'm telling you now, I heard Him saying to me, "Don't judge by the site of your eyes, close your eyes and see with your spirit!"

Or I guess you could say, "Don't look at the natural aspect of your situation, close your eyes and see who I've given you spiritually." Sometimes our eyes can cloud the issues in our lives and keep us from seeing what is really there. Many times in life, our natural vision can mislead us. Our senses can be manipulated by things like media, our past experiences and even social environments which could influence our thoughts and decisions. A word that came to us as a congregation by Pastor Mike once was this, "Just because it looks like you're losing doesn't mean that you are." Well, if that's true you can't dismiss the fact that, "Just because it looks like you're winning doesn't mean that you are, either." I think these two points can establish one thing, "DON'T MAKE YOUR SOLE DECISION ON WHAT IT LOOKS LIKE." Pastor's point is that it can look as if it's going wrong but be going right and I'm just saying this also means that a situation can look as if it's going right in the natural but actually be going wrong."

Related to Meriam, I don't have enough time to go into the quality of woman my wife is. It would be a book within itself to begin to tell you just who and what she is, and all I have to say is that if there is any such thing as a total package then that would describe her. I guess you could just go to Proverbs 31 and see her picture there. However, the only way I could get past my own pre-conceived notions of who I believed in my own wisdom the person would be instead of Meriam was to see her in the spirit and not just with natural eyes. It was what the situation looked like not her physical looks.

In my eyes, she was the wrong age. In my eyes she wanted children, and I thought I was done with that although internally I missed the fact that I didn't have my children with me. These were the issues that I couldn't get my head around. I had to see this spiritually. That could mean a lot of things to anybody, but I knew what it was saying to me. Since then, this revelation has become a major point in my ministering when speaking to singles on the subject of seeking relationships. Now it makes all the sense in the world for me, but then it was a new thing. If you can close your eyes and see the foundations under that person's life first, then you have an understanding as to who they really are in their hearts. However, if you close your eyes and realize the things you see are the wrong foundations in their lives, then you know who they really are.

How many times have you seen the situation where a person is in a relationship and on the outside everything looks great, but if you really drill into what that person believes and how they live their life you find fundamental foundational problems. Luke 6:47-49 says, "Whoever comes to me and hears my sayings and does them is like this: he is like a man which dug deep, and laid the foundation on a rock." But verse 49 says, "But he that hears, and does not do them is like a man that without a foundation built a house upon the earth." So, when you close your eyes all you see is the foundation of a person's life, not the house. Just the ground the house of that person's life is on. By using these scriptures, you can either see a person using the Word of God as the principle platform for their lives or they don't.

Believe it or not, it has been proven that by closing some natural senses the body has the ability to cause other senses to grow stronger. When you challenge yourself to not see naturally you're forcing yourself to see the base elements of a person with your spirit. There are things that could stick out in a person's life if you're only focusing on what their lives are standing on. Honesty, integrity, a true love for God, kindness and a desire to protect you and your name are just a few of the things you should see as you see them in the spirit. Even as a man that's been married for now almost 15 years my desire today is that my wife can close her eyes and see me as a man of integrity and having a heart for God. As you may realize, without the Word as our base, we could lose foundational focus on our own lives, but something equally important is the true focus in the life of your potential mate. If we lose the truth of what's most important in people, we can get distracted by other things that can hide who they are. We are all spirits and we can get caught looking at the house and not see the fundamental foundation of the life of the person or if the walls of that house are sound.

CHAPTER FIVE

"So how do we Move Forward with our Future?"

"I WILL NOT ALLOW MY PAST TO STOP OR HINDER ME FROM MY FUTURE."

This statement sounds like it has nothing to do with the choosing or the finding process, but in fact, if this is not drilled into your thinking, it can be the most detrimental aspect of you getting to the life that you desire. I've been a pastor now for almost 15 years, and I can honestly say that the number one issue with most of those who lack the ability to go forward and enjoy life is usually the ability to let go of some aspect of a hurtful or damaging past.

As Christians, if we didn't have a past then there would be nothing to overcome. Oddly enough for me this little bit of information came near the end of my journey of reaching my now 15 years and counting marriage. You are getting the benefit of a trail already traveled, and it's not leading you to a dead end. You can almost see the image of some type of person walking with you everywhere you go and continually reminding you of the things that happened that hurt you, disappointed you, scared you, was said to you that formed your image of who you are or who you're not or even abused you. For every single one of us is a past and we can't just act as if it's not there. We're not into the meat of the process of finding and choosing, but this is the dream killer.

It's funny because I heard the Scripture hundreds of times but until you have to actually do it you don't quite get it. Philippians 3:13 says, "I count not myself to have apprehended: but this one thing I do, forgetting those things which are behind, and reaching forth unto those things which are before, I press toward the mark for the prize of the high calling of God in Christ Jesus."

Now, how do you forget? That's a great question. You see, you can forget where you put your keys or even forget where you parked your car; those things happen all the time, but somehow I don't think this is referring to those things when it says, "Forgetting those things." I think there are two kinds of forgetting.

First, forgetting by accident such as those car keys, that hat or as my son has found out, those glasses, which should always have a special place otherwise you may end up having to get another pair or call the dealership to order a new set of keys. None of us need practice in this type of forgetting because it happens involuntarily. There is some discomfort involved in this forgetting in that you think a little about choosing a good place for them the next time.

Then there's the second forgetting, this one is not automatic and is not accidental. This forgetting is on purpose and is usually connected to something that has brought a great challenge in your life. The reason this forgetting is such a challenge is because this event has been life altering and has been burned into your life almost like a tattoo on your body. This could be a thoughtless decision that has caused a life-long feeling of regret, shame or even feelings of a lack of trust in your own ability to make decisions. I believe this type of forgetting of your past is the place that most, if not all of us, are either frozen in time to or have taken head on and overcome things to move forward.

I had come to that place of knowing that Meriam was the one that God had chosen as the right one for me. I may come back later and talk about the signs but for right now I need to stay with this point. It was time to pull the trigger and I guess to be honest I had run several times during our dating process because I wanted to make sure I gave myself as much time as I felt I needed. I had come to a sense of discovery being alone with God that I didn't want to mess up.

Another thought for me at that time was "I'm a little scared do this again". You see by this time I didn't really trust myself for a life-long decision and that was the best thing that could have happened. My pastor always says, "Knowing what I know now, I wouldn't pick my mate, I would let God do it." Pastor has a great marriage but says he had a bad one and now he has a great one with the same women.

Meriam and I seeing each other had gone on for at least 3 years from the very beginning of us meeting one another and I knew very early that she was special but there was this last step to take. That last step is the step to that place of victory beyond the past that everyone has to take when overcoming the past. Some face the past head on and conquer everything that comes along with it but many never do. This battle is not just about relationships and choosing or finding a mate. This battle is a part of everyone's life. For me, this barrier was the only thing left. I'm not sure if I'm really getting this down as well as I need to, but I'm just going to keep going. It had to be God that dropped this into my spirit because I know I'm not this smart.

Out of my spirit I said something that was the deciding factor for me and it clearly showed that I was ready to move on with my life. "I will not allow my past to stop or hinder me from getting to my future." I can't say what this means for you to hear these words, but I can tell you what this said to me. I was faced with the realization that if I didn't push past my fear of what had happened to me in my past regarding marriage and relationship I would never be able to get too the great relationship that was ahead for me.

That's easy to say but what does that mean? It means I couldn't let the fear of the same thing happening again in my next marriage stop me from trying marriage again. For the average person this is called The Great Wall of "Don't ever go back." This attitude locks a person in their past forever never allowing them to cross over to the promise of the future. The problem with this is you are forever stuck in your past. You are making your decisions based on the hurt of your past and that never moves you forward. Here's why a closer walk with God is important. You are not the same person anymore. You don't think the same therefore you are using a different mind to close the deal. So the reality of this point is you will never get into your future if you allow the fear of the past to drive your choices and decisions. Here are a few points to make about this area that may help you.

I knew that I was not the same person I was when I made the decision to be married the first time. How did I know that? I was born again! My priorities were not the same. My knowledge base for the purpose of marriage was not the same. I had a saying that ended up being the very thing that got me to my wife and it went like this, "I'm not getting married again until God tells me in this ear and the other one too." That's so funny because boy did he!

My willingness to wait for God to tell me who my wife was did so many things in the process that made this journey develop the right way. I know now that If I had used any other criteria for my decision of getting married I would never had gotten to where I am now with Meriam, (especially the fear of what happened before). This is not just about relationships. I know people who were hurt by a pastor and will never trust another pastor, people who were hurt by a coach and never trust another coach, people hurt by a friend and will not allow anyone else to become a friend. The place of deciding to not allow your past to be the deciding factor is a tall order. You must be determined that you will move on. It's really hard when you still have dealings with your past relationships in any way that could be challenging. Here's the point, if you close your eyes and see with your spirit regarding the person and they are all that you believe for and you have done a good enough job of digging into you, (and you have a word from God on the matter), you can move not without fear but in spite of it. It is trust outside of yourself and having real Faith in God that will allow you to move; not trusting you and not just trusting them. That's right! You will have to trust God more than just believing in that other person. I was set in my spirit that even if it meant not doing it again I was going to wait on God. That saved me.

Even after coming to the conclusion of making the decision to go on with your life your past will still be yelling out to you to run. In that case you go by Faith. I'm not saying ignore the voice of the Holy Spirit saying to you don't move, REMEMBER it's His voice you have put your full focus on. But I am saying you have to know the difference between the voice of fear and the voice of your God given spirit saying that you are determined to move beyond the past.

"Now that I know that I Know"

I know what you're thinking, Hey, What happened after that service when you got that word from God?

The service ended and I'm sure after God speaking through a random member of the group and confirming it by my pastor that I ran over to her and said guess what God said right? Wrong!

I can hear some of you saying, "Boy what's wrong with you?" Well, there was a little get together in one of the condos with food and stuff to close the weekend out before we were to leave that next morning. I had decided to wait until then, and she and I could just walk away so we could talk. But there was a problem with this idea and that was the fact that she didn't come. I waited around and talked and ate and sat but no Meriam. By now I'm almost nervous because I don't know where she is. So, without looking to crazy I went down to the next tower to find out where she was staying. I found the condo that her group was using and knocked on the door and they said, "Come on in!" I said, "Has anyone seen Meriam?" and they said, "I think she's out on the deck," so I said "Thanks."

I asked her what she was doing to kind of make small talk and think she said just enjoying the weather. I had nowhere else to go with small talk, so I just came out and asked her, "Has God said anything to you about me?" Not knowing what to expect and not looking for anything too deep she said something that I'm still shocked about today. With a very calm voice and with a matter of fact she said, "He told me two years ago that you were my husband." I said "WHAT! And you didn't say anything!!?"

I will have to refer you to Meriam's accounts on all that happened in this 2 year period, because I could never begin to tell you what was going on in this women's head and life during the process of what God was doing with me. As you can tell my side of the story is wild enough. She goes on to tell me that when I was leaving for Spain that she was also talking to God about us and that she said that she was giving me two weeks after I returned from Spain to do something. If I didn't do anything related to us, she was going to go on with her life. Without each of us knowing it, we were both talking to God about one another.

I think we both realized at the same time that this day was for the both of us the last thing we needed to see. You see because that day on that deck outside of that condo on that trip was the 14th day back from Spain. That's' right! It was exactly two weeks from the day I got back from the trip. I can't tell you how glad I am to have made it! At this point we discussed our relationship but I now realize that she had no idea what had just happened for me. At this time, she had not heard all the things that had gone on and I didn't tell her everything, only that I believed God was saying the same for me.

I'm not sure if she asked the question or I did but the question came up "What do we do now?" The answer was "let's just walk everything out." What Meriam didn't know that had just happened that day was the fact that for me, it was over. I was settled on the rest of my life as related to relationship. I was so settled that I literally felt a weight lift from off my shoulders and for the first time in my life I could go on with the rest of my life without even thinking about my relational life. I felt free!

I now know that Meriam really didn't understand fully what had taken place, but it would all soon be clear to her as well. Later that day I can recall us going for a walk around the area but this time I wanted to hold her hand and this was totally out before that day. She also rode back with me to Birmingham and the next Sunday I went to pick her up for church as well. All these things I would not do until I was sure that this was the person that God had said, "She is the one"!

A few weeks later I did what every man should do, I went to see her father and asked if he would allow me to marry his daughter. From this point on it was all about letting my two children BJ and Kelsie know what was going on and to ask their permission for me to marry Meriam. They were happy about it and BJ said, "If you didn't marry her, I was going to."

So, there's much more to the story especially if you allow my wife to tell it, but from my view I wanted you to see just how spiritual this process was for me and just how involved God was in this process. I then began to see everything He had taken me through to understand who this person was, and it was by His word that I recognized what was happening. The book of Proverbs had a road map that would help me, and these are some of the very things I've tried to get to you.

CHAPTER SIX

"Men Are Finders"

Men, we are hunters by nature, at least I've heard that a few times from different places. I'm not the first to make that statement, but I can say from a man's point of view that men have the internal drive to go after the goal: and I need to put a footnote in that statement of "when we really desire something" In other words, when there's a reason. Everybody knows that trying to get a man to do something he really doesn't want to do is almost impossible. It took me years to learn that men and women are different and I'm still not at the end of that class. I thought when my wife came to me with an issue from the day on her job or just in general she wanted me to tell her how to solve the problem and end it. Silly me. We were married for at least eight years before I realized she didn't want instruction on how to deal with the problem, she just wanted me to care about how she was feeling and be there for her.

When men have a problem, we go into hunter mode and sit and think of a plan as to how to solve and win over it. What is even more frightening is us so called alpha males who view everything as a competition. I would have to write an entire book on that subject alone. Anyway, men we have to understand that as hunters we don't want to allow our nature to work against us. That's why we need to take on a new nature, the nature of Christ.

Here's an example of my hunting drive at work against me. I'm a fairly young deer hunter and I started about five or six years ago. My family has successfully made the switch from the cow. This past year I went to a really great friend's hunting camp to close out the season. His family's camp is probably one of the best in the country and most folks would do anything to get on it for a hunt. Anyway, it was the close of the season and I needed one more deer to last us until the next hunting season, because we probably eat venison once to twice a week.

On any hunting camp there's always a few rules that need to be considered. Unless you have permission, don't shoot the greatest buck! In my case I'm hunting for food not for trophies, so I wouldn't want to do that and mess up my great chance to be in such a nice place, so I'm just going for does. Well, the other rule for camps is also to not shoot the young bucks as well because you need them to reproduce in the camp.

So I'm in the shooting house, which is top of the line and I'd been there a few times before and actually took my son Brandon the year before to get his first deer. Right around sundown, I'm focused on the front and really, it's kind of strange because I'm not seeing a thing. I hear noise behind me in the brush but didn't pay it any mind. Well, after a while I decide to look behind me and right in front of me were about six does and right behind them was a young buck. Not a trophy but a nice four point. I got excited and without even thinking it through I took him down. Even after telling them I was just going for a doe, "the hunter that wants a buck" took over. I felt bad, and he was fine with it, but I still felt bad about not just taking the doe that was right in front of me. Some of it was my youthful excitement and I guess you could say the other part was the desire to shoot a buck.

Anyway, I said all that to set this part of the book up and explain the statement in the title "Men are Finders." With that said, Let's define the word "find." Let me tell you what it's not. It's not looking under rocks or searching in every club, bar or party to find someone that is to be your wife. By the way, that's not where you find wives anyway. In this book, the word "find" is more like the process of evaluation to see what's there. In a courtroom at the end of a case, the judge turns to the jury and ask a very important question, "Ladies and gentleman of the jury, WHAT IS YOUR FINDING or what is your verdict?" Well, in this case, the process of finding is to apply a series of foundational keys to the person you are considering as a potential, long term partner in life in marriage. I happen to believe that there are many men who really desire to get married and have a family.

This book is for you guys who don't want to waste time on a relationship that lacks real potential. You're building a case on whether you see enough proof to hang in there and look further or in some cases close the deal and purchase this house.

There is a difference in just renting and buying. Some women don't mind being rented (or just dating for the fun of it), just like some men don't mind being a renter. But this book is for those who desire a long-term relationship, and for those who desire to get it right.

Where is this concept of "men are finders" coming from? We'll as I said before, I'm using a guide that's been around for thousands of years—the Bible. As I began do develop my relationship with God, I would spend time daily in the word. Usually, as I've previously stated, I would read the book of Proverbs. The more time I spent in the Word, I began to see that the book of Proverbs is full of cues and do's and don'ts for men and women in relationships. I must admit that I wasn't searching for relationship cues at this time, and maybe that's why I began to see more. Maybe because I had put the mission of just growing in God first I opened the door for God to really come into the personal areas of my life. Remember, if you get personal with God, He will get personal with you.

Did I have a list of things that I wanted to see in the natural regarding my wife? Yes, I did. The things I wanted to see were a woman who loved God and who had character. I wanted to see women that loved kids (even if she did not have them). I wanted to see someone who was kind and was a giver. I even threw 5'7" tall in and a certain weight in my list. But, even though I had that list I put all that on hold for growing in God. As I did my daily reading, I started seeing things in these scriptures that were taking me even deeper into understanding who this person should be. The more I saw the more I would see that it would be a great message for singles, and it is. But what I didn't know is that it was for me as well. It was the guideline that I was to use to get me to the person God had for me. Some of the things God spoke to me I won't share in this book, but only because they are specific to my situation. God has some direct things to say to you about your mate that He will only share with you. These things are specific to who you are and how He plans on the purpose He has for you playing out. Listen, you can pick whoever you want to and probably have a nice life. I'm talking to the ones who are reaching for God's perfect will not just to get together with someone and "maybe" things will work out.

All That Glitters Isn't Gold

Proverbs 18:22 says that "whoso finds a wife finds a good thing: and obtains favor of the Lord." With God's system, this would mean only one thing as far as the word "whoso" is concerned. The "whoso" in this case means the man. Why do I say that? Because the word "wife" could only mean women in God's original order. I'll get to the women being a chooser later. I know women are first, but because of the title I'm going to begin here. Here's a bit of a warning. For men, one of our greatest challenges is the fact that we are sight-driven. You can tell by watching ads on TV when they're going after men. It is common for us to go for the women we like looking at the most. Who wouldn't? Remember earlier I spoke about seeing with the right set of eyes. Nowhere in life does this principle of seeing with the right set of eyes apply more than for us men in this arena. I'm not saying it does not apply for women but it's double important for us. This is what we all need to understand, Satan knows how to counterfeit, and that's what he's best at.

Remember the Bible says satan masquerades as angel of light. In other words, He makes himself look good, but he really is not. It like something that shines on the outside, but on the inside is really dark. All that glitters isn't gold men, so make sure you're your "finding" is not based on just the exterior. Let's give some illustrations to help bring some clarity to this issue.

Guys, let's buy a house!

The Bible says in Proverbs 14:1 that," Every wise woman builds her house: but the foolish, plucks it down with her hands." In contract, Proverbs 2:16-18 (NKJV) talks about a woman that "…flatters with her words, Who forsakes the companion of her youth, And forgets the covenant of her God. For her house leads down to death, And her paths to the dead." Here you have two totally different houses and it's up to you to recognize which one you're considering.

When purchasing a house, most people have a budget, so cost is something you must take into consideration. There are a very few that place themselves in position to be financially prepared for a major purchase like a house; however, I'm not talking about a financial cost. This cost, along with the financial, is related to mental, emotional, and spiritual. For the sake of clarity, we will be using the process of purchasing a physical house as an illustration. We must move beyond just curb appeal, and ask what are the true qualities that this house must have? One question which will make you think through this process is, "what's beneath the surface?"

Don't be blinded by the special features

Sometimes when we look at a potential house for purchase we can get blinded by the special features. Special features can be things on the exterior of the house to make it more attractive. The reality of a great find is the fact that the core is the true essence of the house. What you have as a core will make all the difference, not the features. Special features are designed to make the core values even more enjoyable.

The first home my wife and I lived in was really a nice house. I did a lot of personal things to add to the house itself. I had custom stone placed around the front door arch. I put ceramic tile in all the bathrooms and a bench in every shower. I had an island in the kitchen and I had an extra mini fridge placed in the island just for beverages alone. I wired the house for sound upstairs in all the rooms. Outside I did such a good job on my front yard and hedges that one of my best friends said it looked like Edward Scissorhands did my landscape. These were all great features, but if the core of the house was bad, those things wouldn't matter after I moved in. That's the same with relationships. Her measurements, and how "well endowed" she may be won't matter if her core is bad. Ha-ha!!! What if all that stuff was just rented to stage the house? Oooooh! You know, when they only want to make it look good during the time you're considering the home?

Cracks in the foundation are not good.

Checking for a good foundation is the first place to look before buying a house. The foundation is the platform that everything else stands on. You cannot look at a house and see the foundation, and in most cases, you can't look at a person and see the truth of what they stand for. I think we have all found that out by experience at some point and time.

A good sign that a foundation is not good will be cracks in the walls. Where are we going with this point, you may as? Proverbs 25:28 says, "He that hath no rule over his own spirit is like a city that is broken down and without walls." Having walls or good boundaries will be your first place to check when considering who this person really is. Are there places in her life that you can't go? Are there rooms that are off limits to you? I'm not talking about for a few months. I mean only until you buy the house. Are there things in this women's life that she will not do, and does she establish them up front? I'm not knocking any other plan, but waiting three or four dates or six months before having sex is not God's plan. If that's your choice, then work that and maybe it can work, but it isn't God's design. In this case, you want to see her set the standard of wanting to wait until being married. If she's not willing to wait for you to pay the full price for the house, then that's a crack. Remember, you're finding but she should be choosing! She should be seeing in you that you're willing to do whatever the rule for the day is in order to close the deal. I know what many of you are thinking, "Man, that's old fashioned!" Well, remember what I said in the beginning, the right one has a cost, and if she is the right one it's worth the cost you must pay.

"Time is your greatest asset and safe zone"

Guys, when you cross the line of having sex before marriage, it becomes more than just a relationship, and in many cases, this is the boundary you need to keep for your own protection. Aside from the fact that it's not God's plan for you to cross that line before the wedding, and it's dangerous, it also keeps you away from a scenario of hurting someone and never being able to have a friendship if the relationship does not work. Preserving your position of character is most important.

Whether you know it or not, sex is a commitment that should only be shared by a man and women who have made a decision to begin a new life together as husband and wife. It's not just getting your physical needs met with no strings attached. It's a spiritual commitment. It's a soul commitment. Many women today believe that if she can satisfy a man physically it will cause him to stay with them. The problem with this is that men and women can be satisfied physically and not be connected emotionally. In today's world you have men and women who are gaming on each other thinking that they are sexing their way into a stable relationship, and it doesn't work that way. It's shocking to see these so-called reality shows that have nothing to do with love. The sad part is our younger generation (and even older as well) believes these types of lifestyles, and it becomes their new reality and-a way of life. What I'm saying to you is, sex kills the process that we're discussing, and you can't get to the answers you need without the process.

The attic, what's in the attic?

I know you want to know that this woman has common sense, but does she have spiritual sense? If you want to know the content of the attic, listen to the words that come out of her mouth. Matthew 12:34 and Luke 6:45 really touches on this as a great view into the content of anyone's spiritual mind. Luke says, "a good man out of the good treasure of his heart bringeth fourth that which is good: and an evil man out of the evil treasure of his heart bringeth forth that which is evil: for of the abundance of the heart his mouth speaketh."

If you want to know what any person is about, just let them talk. This is a guide that will also apply to-women in choosing, and there are several keys that will cross over to give some indication as to what this person is all about. The attic, or the mind, is the production zone for who this woman is, and by the way, the Bible also says in Prov. 23:7, as a man thinketh in his heart, so is he, so the concept of thinking like a man but acting like a woman does not apply. Here's a novel idea, think like a woman! I personally believe that God's gift to the man is the women and the last thing we need is everybody thinking like men. That would be a nightmare!!! Has anybody really stopped to see how men (especially ungodly men) think? At the core of this philosophy is manipulation and this is a form of witchcraft. You are looking for authenticity. The mouth and the life should be in alignment together with the Word of God as a way of life. If there is no knowledge of God's word in the attic, the life cannot produce what's not there. This is not just scripture quoting or even church going, because even though these activities are good signs of a foundational life, they are not necessarily signs of Spiritual maturity. The life that walks the talk is a life that has good stuff stored away in the attic. Wisdom is the principle thing!

As I stated before I was in this place in my life of just doing what I needed to do to grow in God. When all of a sudden, I started seeing things in the book of Proverbs that changed my entire life. It went from reading for knowledge base to being instruction on the matter of relationship as a man.

It was the clear process of seeing just what the right women would possess and the wrong women would possess.

"What about the history"

With most homes, you'll discover that if it's not brand new there's a good chance someone just moved out. I'm just saying, why did the last person move out. You should ask the question about past relationships and ask why they ended. You may not get the whole story but it's good just to create dialog on the subject of the past. The truth is, we all have one and it's a good idea to discuss yours as well. Along with that, brothers you might want to check the financial history to see if she's managing her affairs well. Guys, you are not someone's financial savior. Just like she should be watching to see if you can stand on your financial feet without her help, so should you. Don't ask for her financial help! Here's a tough one, even if she offers. Many women think that if she is helping you financially it means that she is proving to you that she really cares, but sometimes it also means that she believes you all are together as a couple. Don't take it. It does not mean that you are full of pride, but it could be a trap that you will have to work out of if the relationship does not work. Don't end up on people's court fighting about a gift that ended up being a loan because it didn't work out.

The Right Women

I already know what you're thinking and you are wrong! I'm not going to Proverbs 31 yet. Let's start with another place. If you look at Proverbs chapter eight you'll see some things that God opened the my eyes of understanding to that I'd like to try and share with you. Verse two is a very important indicator and when I get to the wrong women you will understand why. "She standeth in the top of the high places" This simply means she is not hanging in lowly places that are unbecoming of a woman of grace. Even if she has not reached her full potential, this woman has goals and has set her focus on obtaining the purpose God has for her life.

Verse four says "Unto you, O men, I call; and my voice is to the sons of Man." In other words she's calling out to those who are real men of God. She's not wasting her time with men who are not born again or are not truly living a life that even looks like a man of God. What would these men look like, you may ask? Just watch any current reality show and look at the lifestyle of the men on these shows and you'll have your answer: not those men. But that's for the "Women are Choosers" chapters later.

Verse six says, "Hear, for I speak of excellent things: and the opening of my lips shall be right things." Remember, I said before that you'll be able to tell what's on the inside by what's coming out of her mouth. This text simply says she's not talking a bunch of junk. The only way I can explain that statement at this point is to say her conversation is not confusing or all over the place. We saw before that Proverbs 8:6 says I will speak excellent things; and the opening of my lips shall be right things.

Verse seven goes on to say, "for my mouth shall speak truth; and wickedness is an abomination to my lips." Some things you will not hear come out of her mouth. Profanity, lying, game playing to name a few and maybe I will have a chance to dig into this and other issues at another time, but basically verse eight hits it on the head. It says, "All the words of thy mouth are in righteousness; there is nothing forward or perverse in them." Among other things, that word "forward" means to get ahead of the process. In other words, she is forceful or manipulative in trying the reach her desired outcome for the relationship.

No, she should not propose to you men. She should only be discussing marriage in that it is a desire she has, but not acting as if you are already married beforehand. No, she should not be discussing sex and drawing you in brothers, but we'll look at that when we get to the wrong women. Verse nine in chapter nine says the words that are coming out of her mouth are right things to him that finds knowledge. Verse twelve gives you even more guides to go by. She is prudent and she has the desire to find out about witty inventions.

I have to stop here and talk about my wife Meriam. I have never seen anything like this woman. One of the most impressive things I've ever seen her do is put crown molding in our bedroom; that's right I said crown molding! This goes along with working well with her hands but crown molding? The women God has for you has something that you cannot see on the surface, something that's a blessing for you if you allow God to direct you. These are the exact guidelines that got me here so just keep walking with me as we follow a path for you. Let's continue, verse thirteen says there is a respect for God that causes her to hate evil. This word "evil" means ungodliness. Worldliness is not a part of her lifestyle.

Verse 34 tells you that there is a blessing for positioning himself to hear from this lady, but more importantly, watching and waiting. But the best part can be summed up in verse 35, that the man that finds this woman will find life and not only that, but he will also gain favor from God. This is a confirmation to the opening of our journey.

"Whoso finds a wife finds a good thing and obtains favor of the Lord." So what you find is not a wife in development. This woman of God is a wife when you find her. Sure, some houses need renovation, but the structure is good. Because of my wife, I have fallen in love with HGTV, and she has a love for the shows Fixer Upper and Property Brothers. The one thing that amazes me about whatever these shows begin with as a project, they always make the same statement. It doesn't look very nice right now, but it has a good foundation and what they call "good bones." It's just a matter of changing a few walls or adding a room here or there. Your find will have a good foundation, structure and bones. You have to see past the current condition to really see the true foundation. When the show comes to an end the transformation is in most cases amazing. The truth is that what the finished product is was there all along. The real gift that the shows talents have is to see beyond the surface. There are many more examples throughout the book of Proverbs. I encourage you to take some time and read them on your own. They will bring wisdom to your life, and intimacy in your relationship with God.

When you have found a good woman, you will discover that people who have had a chance to really see and know her will do whatever they can to hold on to her. Meriam was working for the housing authority when we got married and about to have the first of our two sons together, Brandon. We decided that she would not work after having the baby, and take care of Brandon, especially in his first few years. When she took off for maternity leave she let them know that she would not be returning. After a few months they called and told her that they wanted her to come back. We discussed it and agreed that we wanted her to stay home and the company said, "We'll give you a laptop and you can work from home."

Proverbs 3:18 says that "She is a tree of life to them that lay hold upon her: and happy is everyone that retaineth her." Nobody I know of that Meriam has ever worked for has ever wanted her to leave. She has been a blessing to everyone she has worked for and you know how hard that has to be sometimes because not every workplace is a blessing for you. Does a good relationship follow her from her previous jobs? In the book of Ruth chapter 2:11 Boaz told Ruth, "It has fully been shown me all that you have done." It was related to how she conducted herself and the level of her commitment. What is the reputation of this lady? What is the level of her relationships after she moves on in life? You learn more about a relationship many times after the relationship ends.

I chose Auburn University to get my education and to play division 1 football and run track. To me it was a mutual relationship, and in many ways, I became a professional athlete the day my college career began. Our greatest foundation besides the excellent education at Auburn is that motto that "We Are Family!"

It was indeed that during my years on the plains, but remember, I brought something to the table as well. It was after my relationship as a student athlete had ended that I saw the real value of our relationship. I was recruited to work in the office of development in fundraising for about three years, then I became a member of the Board of Trustees and was given the privilege of serving there for twelve years. It was a valuable experience, but it spoke even more about my decision to choose to go to Auburn as a high school senior. This is the point I'm making: it's how you are treated after you have no more eligibility that really tells the type relationship you have. We were in the midst of challenging times during my trustee term, and it didn't come without serious attack. However, I've learned the valuable lesson that no leadership comes without persecution. It comes with the territory. My point is in the end that I have great things to say about Auburn, and I would hope that Auburn has great things to say about me. That's how you want every relationship that occurs to be when and if they end.

So why am I talking about how relationships should be when they end? Because you will see something in the women that's right for you, which will say to you she is willing to cut you loose. This woman will have a strong sense of who she is and will stand strong with inner strength, because she is willing to let you go if you don't meet her standard. Why? Because she is a chooser and will hit the reject button at any time when the relationship is not lining up with her foundation. Not because you made her mad, but simply because you don't line up. A strong women doesn't chase a man, and she doesn't put up with a bunch of nonsense. One thing that really made Meriam stand out to me was the fact that when we didn't talk or see one another she didn't come looking for me.

Ok, I must admit that I was afraid early in our relationship, and I would literally hide from her for weeks at a time. This was mostly because I knew that if we spent more time together we would get serious. I knew right away that she was special. Well, I felt that I needed time to just be alone to know who I was and to dig out as much of my past as I could so the next person wouldn't have to pay the price for my past hurt's, anger and mistakes. This is the interesting thing, she didn't come looking for me, and it actually came to the place that I started saying, Hey! How come this girl is not chasing me? She will have to tell you about what was going on between her and God at that time but for me her strength to stand in her place made her different and stand out. What was she saying by standing in her place of strength? She was saying, in short, that she didn't need me to make it. If you're in a relationship that she is saying to you, "I can't live without you," you are in big trouble, because that place is reserved for God and you can't be God.

I didn't say she's not saying she doesn't want to live without you, I said she's saying she CAN'T live without you. There's a difference. I think I even called her to find out why she wasn't calling me. Of course, there is a balance to everything, but in the end, you need a woman that is independent enough to not have to lean on you just to stand up. That means she's standing with God as her strength to live out each day. A woman who values herself would never fight another woman over a man! Why? Because if he's not smart enough to see her value and knows who he wants in his life, then he's not worth having. She will hit the reject button and wait for the next candidate. Women of strength don't settle. Now brothers, the whole mindset has to change, and you have to raise your standard to fit. That's what's missing in today's culture. I spoke to a group of young students and asked them what was wrong with boys today. The one thing the young ladies said about boys was that somehow, they have successfully convinced the girls that they need them to succeed. Unfortunately, many of the girls have accepted this, and have in turn set very low or no standards for the boys they get involved with. It's not just the young generation that have made that mistake, it's singles in all generations.

The Wrong Women

Ok, we spent a little time discussing the qualities that you should look for in a potential mate. I have to say in this process of finding that it is very possible that you will see some things that are not in this particular book that God will show you. Why is that you may ask? God is specific, and He knows more about you than even you understand. The keys I'm giving you in this book worked for me, but I believe God wants to talk to you about your keys as well. I believe this book is to open you up to, not just what God is saying, but how God speaks. This book will also tune you in to the place in your spirit where God will reach you. Chapter five of Proverbs begins by validating the importance and safety of wisdom.

Verse three starts out just like any other meeting of two people with flattery; however, in this case this flattery is insincere or excessive praise. Flattery is not just saying nice things to a person it's what you might call "over kill." Only you can judge where that line is. Everyone loves praise, but, in some cases, it can blind you because emotionally, you need attention. Often the attention is desired because you don't get it anywhere else.

I know you love hearing about yourself, but sooner or later the conversation needs to go deeper than just how wonderful you are. In the next few verses of that chapter you can see something that I believe is a solid issue. If you read verses 7-8 you can see a foundational problem with this woman. Her goal is the search for an ignorant young man. Her goal is not as much one who lacks common sense knowledge as much as it is a man that has no godly wisdom. Brothers, you know if you truly have the wisdom of God. You know whether or not you have the word of God as your base or if you run your life with Godly wisdom. I know we're talking about the qualities you need to see in her, and this is the one you want the most. If she is choosing you, is it because she sees in you a man of wisdom or a fool?

Let's go into a touchy area, dress. Every man wants to see a nicely-dressed woman, and we all have our own taste as to what that means. There is a place where the focus of dress is to drive your attention to the physical attributes of a woman and not the true foundation of the house. Let's go back to the house buying again. A new paint job, changing the light fixtures, showing off the nice whirlpool tub and the nice surround sound system and throwing in a nice beer cooler could really be enticing but those things distract you from the fact that termites are eating the frame away. What I'm I saying? Every woman should care about her looks and will dedicate time and money toward that as an agenda, but if its purpose is to get you to focus more on the looks than the content of the foundation of who they really are, then the real substance is being covered.

Remember, you shall not judge by the sight of your eyes. Proverbs 7:10 drives it home by pointing out that she is a woman with the attire of an harlot. If you can't tell the difference between the women that is on the corner and the women that is dressing for success, then there could be another problem. As challenging as the topic of how she dresses is, I'm about to go deeper. It says in vs11 that she is loud and stubborn. I think being loud speaks for itself, but stubborn is a tough one to get past for anyone. It goes on to say that her feet abide not in her house. It's ok to want to go to events that are going on and be outgoing person, but a woman that is always partying and going out is another issue. If she never wants be in a place where she tends to home matters or just takes time to rest and to devote her time, attention and resources to developing herself is not a good sign. Chapter seven, verse twelve says that she's broke. When you're always on the go and focused on going to everything that's going on at every corner, "being without (or broke) is the usual result.

I'd like to close this section out for you men with a final sign that she is not the women for you. In Proverbs 7:18 she says, "Come let us take our fill of love until the morning," fellows, for those of you who don't know, that is sex! This woman is not only open to the idea of having sex, but she will be the one to bring it up as an option. Remember, I told you earlier that your protection from hurt and future relationship as friends is connected to not getting physically involved. But even more that that it can protect you from the danger of early death. In 7:25-26, it says, "Let not thy heart decline to her ways, go not astray in her path. For she has cast down many wounded." Yes, many strong men have been slain by her but 7:27 tells the end results. "Her house is the way to hell, going down to the chambers of death." The lie today that young girls are led to believe is that they give the sex and they can get the man. They may get the man, but only for a season. Ladies, what you get is a man that is living by his flesh, but a man that is controlled by his flesh is not led by his spirit.

Everything today in media is driving society to live by your feelings and by your appetites. A major indicator that she is the wrong one is that the physical things of life are far more important than the spiritual. How will you know that? Out of the abundance of the heart the mouth speaks. The woman in Proverbs chapter seven talked about her bed being covered with tapestry and carved works and topped off with fine linen of Egypt. She spoke of her bed being perfumed with myrrh, aloes and cinnamon. Everything about this woman was set to appeal to the physical senses of a man, but if you notice there was nothing about her that was designed to appeal to the spiritual foundation of her life, nor the life of the young man in which she was encountering. Men, you have to close your eyes so your judgment is not clouded. Verse 26 proves the she has a long history of men whose lives have been destroyed. Not only that, but she is known to cheat. Proverbs 7:19, shows that as a matter of fact, this woman is married.

Chapter five, verse six of Provers says, "Her ways are moveable, that you can't know them." First, this says you don't know what this woman is doing. She's hard to figure out and more than anything else, she's unreliable. There is nothing worse that a person you can't count on. Guys, if you go to Proverbs 9:13, it says the wrong women for you is foolish and clamorous, which means aggravating. It also goes on to say that she knows nothing. Remember, you're looking for a woman with knowledge.

Over in Proverbs 12:4 (again, read this book – it is FULL of wisdom), it speaks of that fact that a virtuous woman is a crown to her husband: but the woman that makes him ashamed is rottenness in his bones. If you can't take this woman anywhere and her be with you in every arena, then she's not the one for you. Again, I know that I could go on with these, but my point is to get you to look in the Word and see for yourself. I guess you could say these examples are helping you to see with your spirit as you look in the Word as well as while you walk through the process of finding the one God has for you. I didn't want this to be just another recipe book. There's nothing wrong with keys and steps, but I wanted this book to be more of a personal experience that you can plug into your spirit and better understand how the process was created and not just hear a formula without the spiritual life that makes it work.

As an NFL player, the one thing we were taught to better understand our game plan was for us to know not only what our plays were, but we also needed to know why we did what we did on every play. You didn't get the ball every play but understanding why you did what your assignment was without the ball gave meaning to the full purpose of what you were doing each time. Hearing my story will help you know how the process came about, which helps you to know why as well as how. Guys, you need God's help to get you to a place of success in relationships. I know that if I had not trusted God totally, I would have not made it.

CHAPTER SEVEN

"Women are Choosers"

Where in the world did this idea come from? In some cases, but not all today, you choose, find, rope, drag, trap or any other technique you can use to get a man. I'm not saying that any of this is you, but I am saying that the role of women and men getting together has become an interesting process. Now you have websites specifically designed to help match people up. We need to understand that whatever you do, don't use reality TV as your pattern. Ok, I guess by now you can tell I'm not a fan of these shows. Like I told you before I'm only giving you an option. I think many people feel that they have no choice in what and how they go about connecting with the person they share their life with.

I heard from my teacher that the word of God is pregnant and that it's always giving birth to deeper understanding. I think it's happened to me more times now than I can remember, but this time it has been the birth of this entire process which again has taken me 15 or so years to capture. If you're not a Bible person or even a Christian I can try and explain this concept; which is a little like watching a movie over and over again. Every time you watch it, you see something you didn't see before. My favorite movie is "Dances with Wolves," and I've seen it at least 50 times. Now, if I see something new it really shocks me because I've seen it so many times, but without fail, I catch something new. I think it's said that no matter what you are doing, just for a split second you look away and in that short time you miss something.

Now maybe that point can help you understand why the Bible says that faith comes by hearing and hearing, because we may have missed something. So this is a reminder to ask yourself "The First Question," which is "Am I Ready?" Remember, I'm writing this as an inside view to what God did for me and somehow you'll need to get Meriam's account on this entire experience to see it from the other side.

For the sake of staying with the mission we can just see it from my side. If you are not a Christian, that's ok; just find a time when nobody is around and take a look at Proverbs 31. This one chapter will make you think. Talk about superwoman! The woman described in this chapter of the Bible is a picture of every real man's dream and every woman's desired goal to achieve. Now let's get something clear, I understand that not every woman has the desire to be a wife, and before you read this chapter you need to understand that this is the picture of a woman who does it all. I, like most, have always seen this as the model, and to be honest it's been a pretty impossible goal to find such a woman (until I met Meriam). I know what you're thinking, "He's just bragging on his wife." I am, but if you know my wife, you know it's 100 % true. Of all the scriptures in Proverbs 31 that speak about this woman, hidden in the middle of all these guidelines of the perfect woman are 3 small points that peek over into the kind of man that she chose. These 3 scriptures inspired the book and inspired the view that women are choosers. If this is the picture of the ultimate woman, then you have to look at the type of man the ultimate woman would choose. God does nothing by accident, and the fact that there were 3 points made about the man that was by this woman's side was enough for us to see into their relationship.

I have to say that it was this understanding that caused me to realize that I had to now look at myself to see if I would measure up to a super woman's choice. The rest has become history. I've begun this journey of which you have become a part if you're reading this book. Here we go:

Ladies, it's your job to choose. I heard it said once that you can tell the type of person someone is by the kind of person they choose for a husband or wife. I would like to think that my wife chose according to her super status. Ha, at least in my mind she did exactly what the virtuous woman did. There is a long list of things to point out as it was for the men's process for finding but the difference is that you will choose as they come into your life. You have the choice of spending time with this guy or pushing the reject button and moving on.

The word "choose" as defined by dictonary.com, means to select from a number of possibilities or to pick by preference. Remember you are not doing the finding, your role is the make the right choice. If you want to go out looking for a man to be in your life, that's your decision. I'm only showing you another way. Here is another question for you before we get into who that person may be. Do you look like the Proverbs 31 woman to him? Can you take a realistic view of this virtuous woman and say, "That's me?" Right here we have to do a little soul-searching to ask a serious question. Are you the best that you can be? I'm sure some of you are saying, "My house has been on the market way too long!" Well, whatever you do, don't lower the price! We see way too many bad experiences of women who have lowered standards just to make a sale.

My wife is a whiz at many things. One thing she will not

move on however is how to prepare a house to sell. We sold our home in Birmingham in less than a month when even we thought it would take a lot longer. Most of that was the favor of God, but a lot of it was what went into getting the house ready. I tell you, I am not a handy man, but by the time we were done we not only had a much more presentable house, but I came away feeling like I was Tim the Tool Man. She had me change light fixtures, shower doors, door handles, paint the walls, and change counter tops just to name a few things. I guess you can understand where I'm going. There must be an honest evaluation of what's going on with you. Are You the best that you can be? We're using the Proverbs 31 women right, well then you need to shoot for that and not just settle for where you are. Remember I'm talking to those who are not willing to settle where they are. The Bible says in 1 Samuel 16:7 that "man looks at the outward appearance, but the Lord looks at the heart." As a man I can say to you that somebody is always looking at the outer appearance. What this means is that it's not just what kind of clothes you wear or how "fine" you are, but it's also how you carry yourself. Review the man's guidelines and locate yourself. Which list are you on?

The next thing I want to mention before getting into the 3 points in Proverbs 31 involves something my wife once said to me. After we were together while we were discussing this whole process, and she said there was a point when she was very frustrated about the fact that I was not committing to the relationship and she went to God about me. That's funny because I went to God about me too! She said that she asked God, "Why is he not spending more time with me?" Well, she said that God came right back to her and asked her, "How much time are you spending with me?" She would have to give you this issue more discussion than me, but she said that she realized her focus off. Instead of being focused on God, she realized her focus was all about me.

Well, even that gave my ego a bit of a hit, I wanted her to have related to the relationship that way. God wanted Him to be her main focus, not me. I was holding back because I was afraid to leap "all in" due to the past experience with my previous marriage, and it was mainly due to a lack of trust in myself making the right decision more than anything else. So I would see her briefly then run for the hills to stay away from her, and in the process, she had become frustrated. Ladies, this can help some of you understand that many times there are some things being worked out that you need to allow to unfold. Instead of pressing the issue you should allow God to handle it for you. It's funny that during this time her mom, who has gone on to be with the Lord, said (I found out later), that I was wishy-washy. I'm sure I did look pretty much that way based on what was going on at the time, but I'm very proud of the fact that Mrs. Helen was here long enough to see me commit to her daughter.

The truth is, God was dealing with me on ministry as well as dealing with me about Meriam. I told you about the weekend in Florida with the singles and how God had finally reveled to me about her being my wife. Well, this is what I didn't tell you about how we got officially engaged. I told you about the trip to Spain and what happened there. And you've read about how I spoke to my pastor on the singles' trip and how I got that Word from God that said "Judge not by the sight of your eyes." Well, here's the rest of the story. That afternoon there was a get together to eat on the last day before we were to begin packing to head back to Birmingham. I talked to friends and ate and sat around, and Meriam wasn't around. Finally, I had it and I could not go on any longer.

As I stated earlier, later that evening I went to the condo where she and other ladies were staying and asked if she was in. They said she was out on the deck. She and I sat out on the deck at that condo to talk and I didn't know really what to say, but just thought I would start the conversation off with a blunt question. Has God said anything to you about me? Her answer to me was shocking, She said, "God told me two years ago that you were my husband." I said, "WHAT? Two years ago, and you didn't tell me!" The truth is, she wasn't supposed to tell me. I had to hear that bit of information for myself! That's the mistake that many women in the body of Christ make. They go straight to the person and tell them what God said.

I proceeded to talk to her, and as I stated before, the most amazing point about this encounter is that she said, "I had told the Lord that I was giving you two weeks after you got back from Spain and if nothing happened between us then I would just move on." The day I came to her condo was day 14th. It was the last day she had set between her and God. Can you say what God has for you is for you? How could that just happen? How could that just be an accident? The truth is, it wasn't. After all that had occurred between my process with God in the last few years and about this woman and after knowing that He had said to me that she was my wife, this conversation sealed the deal. I don't think that even she realized fully understood what had taken place after that meeting. For me it was over. I literally felt a relief and a weight lifting from off my shoulders. From that moment on it was settled for me related to relationship.

It was amazing how this whole thing happened, and it's your turn to see what God wants to do for you. I asked her

"Well, what do we do now?" Not sure if she asked that or me but for me, we were engaged. I suddenly realized that this was a plan. I know what you're thinking: *Where's the ring?* Well a few weeks later I formally proposed to her at one of our favorite restaurants. I went in early and set up a scene for the waiter to come up to us and say that we were the millionth customers and that we would have a free meal. Because we didn't drink, I gave them a bottle of sparkling apple cider to say they had in the back if we wanted that instead of alcohol. I called her family and some friends who went to the place early and hid while we went through the process of me proposing. It was so funny because when the waiter came and said everything and left, I told Meriam I was going to tell them that we should get our meal free too for being the special customers that we were. She was begging me to please not do that. He returned with the apple cider, and after he took our order and left I reached in my pocket and pulled out the ring, got down on one knee, and proposed. The family came out from the back, and it was officially done. I would like to mention that I asked her father beforehand and also told my parents, as well as met with my son and daughter and told them as well. The conversation with my kids was critical. I was a package deal, and that had to work or nothing would. That's another story as well.

Now, let's talk about the signs for the women.

"I SHALL RETURN"

You may be experiencing the same relationships over and over again with different men. Well, this portion will maybe help you understand a little better as to why that is. First, I want to give you a scripture that may make sense to you or may not when I say it, but after I explain you should get it. In Matthew 12:43-44 (NKJV) you will see a description of a demonic spiritual attitude.

It says in verse 43, "When the unclean spirit is gone out of a man, he walks thru dry places, seeking rest, and finding none".

Verse. 44 then says, "I will return into my house from which I came out; and when he finds it empty swept and garnished,"

Verse 45, "He then takes with himself seven other spirits more wicked than himself, and the last state of that man is worse than the first. Even so shall it be also unto this wicked generation."

I picked up a really bad habit of drinking many years ago, that's a long story but the good news is I've been delivered now for over 20+ years. The reason why I'm bringing this up is because the spirit of God asked me a question related to these scriptures. The question was "So, how many more are you going to let back in?"

You see, in order to make myself believe that I was not addicted to drinking, I would stop for 21 days, then go right back. The only problem is that when I went back I always seemed to drink more. So, this helped me to understand the spiritual principle behind why most people's addictions got worse when they would go back.

That's not really why I'm talking to you about this. I'm showing you this because of the early part of these scriptures. The part that says, "I shall return."

I talked a little about closing your eyes and seeing with your spirit. One thing you will need to do is to pay close attention to the next guy and be careful that once you have gotten out of a bad relationship, you're not about to connect with the same spirit in a different package. When you start seeing by the spirit and not by the appearance you will be able to see if it's the same guy just dressed in a different look.

That's why many times women say, "I'm not going to go for a guy that looks like this or that" but in the end you have the same problems. It's not the look of the guy that was the problem; it was the spirit in the guy. It is a truth that in life you will not graduate to the second grade if you never pass all the tests in the first grade. The first test you will need to pass when you are at the point of choosing is the test of seeing past the exterior of the person and actually seeing them by the spirit. That will be your new standard. If you continue to use the same standards as before, just remember these words, "I shall return" is going to get in line just to see if he can get back in again. Sure, you want to like some things about the person from the outside, but just remember the outside is just the house. The real person, that's the spirit of the person, is on the inside.

The First Sign

The first sign for you ladies is in Proverbs 31:11. It says "The heart of her husband does safely trust in her, so that he shall have no need of spoil". I saw in this that he has a level of trust for his wife that outweighed his pursuit of things and possessions. She was the most valued component in his life. Ladies, can you see this level of trust in the man you are seeing? It's not the trust of staying faithful (and boy you need that), but this is a value trust. He knows that with you in his life something good will happen in both his and your lives.

At our wedding, Meriam and I were given the opportunity to make a face to face public statement to one another. When the time came for me to say something as a statement, I didn't really have to search too deep for what to say. My statement went something like this,

"I don't know where I'm going, and I don't know what I'll be doing, but whatever it is, I want you by my side."

I'm not sure if my wife remembers that, but I sure do. Ladies, this is the level of trust you want to see in the guy that's for you. It's the first sign of a quality man. I can only give the guidelines, but you have to apply the rules for yourself. The treasure is you, not just what you bring. I'm not saying that you shouldn't bring a wealth of blessings to the table, but that man needs to see you as the blessing. My wife has brought way more to the table than I ever knew was coming, but the real gift is Her. Who Meriam is, what she stands for and her spirit, make her being with me such a blessing. Do we disagree? Yes! Do we go to God to talk about things going on in our lives? Yep, does she do things that are totally opposite from me? Yep! But, I can close my eyes and see who she is, and she is awesome. She's awesome when I open my eyes too!

THE SECOND SIGN

The second sign is found in Proverbs 31 in verse 23, ""Her husband is known in the gates, when he sits among the elders of the land."

This key is related to the social standing of the man she chose. First you must understand a little about the times in which this text refers. The word "gates" here refers to places of gathering for important issues. You could say these are the places where decisions are discussed and made about many different aspects of life and lives around the city. This does not have to be at the highest level like political positions in government, but it does mean that on some level in the community this man is known and respected. Respect is not bought, it's earned. The arena for which the respect is given to this person matters greatly. In this text, it would represent areas of work, business, and or community service. No man of low character can gain respect in the gates. The word elders represents the leaders and only people of respect can hang in this environment. He may not be the leader, but he has respect of those even in leadership places. This could be on his job, at his church or even in the neighborhood. This is not talking about holding some powerful position, because you can be in a powerful position and lack character. This is the presence of respect at some level. I know this may not sound like something to focus on when choosing a mate, but I'm just showing you what the top woman in the Bible chose. I'm only saying that there is a reason why this quality was exposed about her choice.

THE THIRD SIGN

Finally, Proverbs 31:28 says, "Her children arise up and call her blessed; her husband also, and he praises her."

Listen, only a man of good strong self-esteem can praise his wife. Show me a man that can say good things about his girlfriend or wife to his friends and to anyone and everyone openly, and I will show you a man that knows who he is and is not competing for attention or acceptance. In today's world it has become somewhat popular to say funny and even negative things about our spouses or girlfriends too our friends. You're not the old lady, the ball and chain, the baby momma or any of that stuff. This text says he praises her. That word praise means to lift up and to set on a high place.

Right here I need to flip the script to make this point. In Proverbs 4:8 you get a glimpse of something God showed me about how a man should treat his wife, or I guess you could even say girlfriend. It simply says, "Exalt her, and she shall promote thee: she shall bring thee to honor, when you embrace her." Verse nine says, "She shall give to your head an ornament of grace: a crown of glory shall she deliver to you."

This is instruction and insight for the men, but right now I'm making my point for you, ladies. This man lifts you up, he looks to say and do good things for you. He speaks well of you in public (and in private), and without shame. He brags on you. Again, these are the guidelines you should use in making your choice. If he only wants to see you in private, then what are you doing? I know it's done, but don't make yourself some secret side chick. That means that you have no respect for yourself. You may be getting some money and getting some things, but the reality in that situation is that you are nothing more than a fee for some person's playtime. If you're ok with that then this book is not for you anyway. Here's a truth, real true relationships are not everyone's goal.

Listen, if "what you do" is the basis for a relationship, and not who you are, that's not a relationship - that's a business deal. Jesus paid everything up front for a relationship, not a business deal. The right guy will take a chance on losing in order to win.

"CHOOSE A MAN THAT PREPARES"

Proverbs 24:27 "Prepare thy work without, and make it fit for thyself in the field; and afterwards build your house."

If you've ever sat in our church, sooner or later this scripture comes up. Now ladies I'm going to use this from my perspective, but it's setting you up for the understanding as to what to see when choosing a mate.

I used this process in two separate situations. The first time was in the development of the "Buffalo Connection", a wing place that I started in Auburn, AL. I had no idea what I was walking out, but it was the framework for what I've learned. The second time I worked this process was related to this book, and what I believe was the final stages of activating my faith for my wife. I told this story in one of my "Power Hour" sessions at Buffalo Rock, which was our company-wide Bible study, and one of the women in our Bible study jumped up with tears in her eyes and said, "I WANT ONE OF THEM!" (as in a man that went to such lengths to prepare for his wife). I recognized then what I shared that day, and what I'm about to tell you was something very special.

It's so interesting how the Spirit of God led me through this discovery even without me knowing it.

These were the days before I got the signs that Meriam was my wife. I was in the process of getting back on my feet after moving to Birmingham and beginning my job at Buffalo Rock. One of the things that I wanted to do was to get a house. Getting that house was for me, but even more so it was for my two kids who had seen me go from apartment to a room in another person's home to again another apartment. I feel it was important for them to see me recover. It was a planned surprise; I'd been working on the plan for a few weeks after I moved in. It was set that when I went to pick them up from Atlanta I asked them if they minded if we stopped by a friend's house to drop off some papers. When the day came they said sure! When we pulled up to the house I looked at them and said "Welcome home!" It was a great surprise for them and a very good feeling for me to see their reaction.

Anyway, it was in this home that I was growing in God and working on the steps I needed to move on with the next chapters in my life. As a matter of fact, my relationship with the Lord had grown so strong while in that last apartment, that I stayed in it just one more night after moving all my things into this new house. I even slept on the floor. I don't know maybe it was to say thanks for meeting me here or maybe I was a little scared that I would lose what we (me and Jesus) had. Either way, In the process I grew spiritually, and my life was a life of relationship not religion. The faith message became a way of life and now I'm starting to work the word in my everyday life. Now that I reflect on this point, it was even before I got the word that I was ready for marriage.

I took this word in Proverbs 24:27 and began to prepare myself without. I bought a cotton ball holder and put it in the bathroom on the other side of the sink from the one I used in the master bath. I put a lotion dispenser on that side with the cotton ball holder. I put a Q-tip holder on that side as well, but it's important to say that nobody was coming in my bathroom at that time but me. I had two closets, but I only put my stuff on one side. I had a nice queen-sized bed, but I only slept on one side. I had really nice bedroom furniture, but I would only use one row of drawers and left the others empty. And finally, I had this really nice two-car garage, but I only parked on one side. Why did I do all of that? By faith I was preparing for what I wanted. I didn't know who it was for sure at the time that was coming, but I know this, when they showed up it was going to be a place ready for them. Not just the house itself, but a place in that house. And not just a place in that house, but even more importantly, a place in my life.

Ladies, a man that's serious is preparing. At the end of the day you can see that he is getting ready for what he has faith for and if a man does not have faith working for anything coming in his life he's not for you. Just ask him this really telling question, "What do you have faith for? What he says will pretty much tell you everything you need to know. This will work unless you know nothing about faith yourself. Listen, faith is an action word and you should be able to see some type of faith process at work in his life. For those of you who are not Christians and don't understand this comment then consider this; God uses faith as His way of directing us to keep us from getting tricked by the enemy by using your own senses against you. In the natural state of things if you as the women are making all the plans, picking all the timelines, pushing him toward any serious commitments related to the two of you building a future together, then get used to it. If he does not prepare now, he will not prepare later.

I believe that faith was a part of my getting my gift from God in Meriam, but you should be looking at this example from the other side. Think about what Meriam was seeing in me as she was choosing. I would like to talk a little to those of you who are the smart ones, you know, the ones that are saying, "I'll just do this part and skip all the other stuff." Well, that won't work. Why you may ask? Think of all the other things that I learned and dealt with myself just to get to that point.

It's not just about whom to choose, it's also about being found. There are two sides to this thing and most people avoid the side they stand on. The first question comes up again, "Am I ready" well I'm about 90% sure that the answer for many of you today is "No."

Like R. Kelly's famous song starts out "My mind keeps telling me no, but my body is telling me yes." Don't jump the gun. Allow God to really do the work in you that needs to be done. The rule to prepare is for you too. That's why this text is so powerful. You want a man that prepares, but you really need to take this time to prepare yourself. Remember, this time you're doing this thing differently because you want different results. If you're one of the proactive folks who's just reading up on relationships and have not been through a lot, then this will be a wonderful road map to keep you down the road of relationship success. But if you're searching for the answer to why it's not working for you like I was, then let this book help you. There's one more area he will be preparing for, "You." I have to say that I can only share this from the perspective of where I was at the time. I was not playing around, and I was fully decided on not being by myself and hoping for someone to share my life with. I wasn't broadcasting to the world that I wanted to be married, but I was serious as to what I wanted in my own heart.

It's kind of strange to say this when I'm sure you heard me say that I was running from Meriam. Well that's true, but I knew I needed some time to get myself together and to jump right into a relationship with her at that time was not good timing for me. Remember, along with that point that I still didn't know she was the one. Anyway, if you listen to him and watch him he's not just talking about the future, he's planning for it. He's making decisions that will be clear that he will be prepared to start a life with someone.

One of the clearest areas you will see the answer to the question of preparation is in his finances. You may not be fully exposed to his financial life, but you will clearly see his spending patterns and know if he has a bunch of debt with no regard for the future. If he is borrowing money from you then that is not a good sign. Is all his spending on his play toys or hobbies without thinking about savings? By the way, don't be so quick to start buying him things and running to the rescue with your checkbook to prove that you are ready to give what you have.

This is one of the biggest mistakes women make as it relates to relationships. You can't buy love, but you can sure buy big problems. Take the time to see if he can stand on his own two feet financially. Does he have children? If he does, does he pay child support? If he's avoiding child support and says he sends money when it's needed, that is a big red flag. Child support keeps personal issues between the parents to a minimum. There can be no manipulation of kids and visitation with parents and or money and it protects the father from being controlled, which also creates a bad situation for everyone. It also keeps the father from holding money over the head of the mother as a form of control. No, he wants the freedom of moving forward with his life as well as taking care of his parental responsibility even if it's at an ordered cost. I'm not happy at all about going through this personally, but I can say that I made every payment for 18 years as ordered by the courts and even did above what was required. Money is challenging enough between two people with good sound practices, so take the time to really check this area out.

"He Protects You"

This world is full of danger. You only need to turn on the TV or open your smart phone to see examples of that. One of the best signs you need ladies to know if this guy has the right stuff is his willingness to desire to protect you. Sure, it's to protect you physically, but it's really more than that. The kind of protection I'm referring to is the kind of protection that's even more valuable than your possessions.

My dad is a great man. I've learned a lot of things from him along the way, and I'd love to say that I've done a great job at walking all the lessons he's taught me. The truth is I feel that I've missed a bunch of those early in life, but thank God I've got more time to get them right. He said something to me really early in my teens that I've never forgotten. He said that the greatest thing we all possess is our name and our word. He said to damage either one of these two things is to make the overall value of who you are equal to zero.

Why am I bringing this up to you ladies? Because this man will do everything he can to protect the honor of your name and the integrity of your word. It will show in how you are treated that one of his main concerns will be to protect the integrity of your name. Now remember, everything in today's society says that living together and sleeping with one another before you are married is ok.

I don't have enough time in this book to get into this point, but I can say that you want him to consider what others are saying about you because of his involvement with you. I know I keep crossing this thing on sex, but one of the greatest ways you can judge whether or not to choose a man is by how he protects your good name in the streets. That's not just about what everybody else might say, but it's what God will say. You as the women of God want to be found.

My wife was absolutely clear on what type of relationship we would have. I also wanted to do everything the right way to be sure that I was giving our marriage every opportunity to work. It took both of us holding each other to the standard we desired related to God's plan. This is the kind of man that you want to choose. You want a man who wants to cover his bases on the physical side of life as well as the spiritual side. He will show a concern about the spiritual aspect of the future that will be ahead. Remember, this man is preparing. He's building a platform for his life that has the right stuff; even if he goes on without you he will be standing strong. That should tell you about the kind of person this man is. He wants to please God more than wanting to please his body. I've told my daughter on several occasions that a real man will protect you. Look for him to protect your body and not look to satisfy himself at your expense. Look for him to live a life that won't drag you into danger or put you in harm's way. If he runs with the wrong crowd he will cut those relationship loose. If he's doing things that are illegal, he will stop (but if he's doing things that are illegal, you need to hit the reject button).

"He Will Exalt You"

"Only a man of self-assurance can promote his wife or anyone else for that matter."

One of the greatest signs of the right guy for you is that he will do all he can to help you be all you can be and to reach your dreams. I was surprised to hear my wife say to me not long ago that she didn't know what her role was in the ministry.

My first thought was that I didn't understand why she would feel that way because she is second in command and vice president of the non-profit organization known as "Living Word Church." She is the executive director for the church and head of the youth ministry and above that she is my wife, which is the unit that God used to put everything we're doing in place. It's amazing that you could be doing all that and she does even more and be feeling that you are missing something as it relates to your personal mission. As her husband, I have to realize that the same inner drive to accomplish what God has put in me is also in her. She's not ungrateful in where she is, but she is not content in where she is. Just like me. as her husband and her friend and as her greatest cheerleader my job is to make sure she is fulfilled.

Proverbs 4:8 says this, "Exalt her and she shall promote thee." That's a pretty good deal because it also says the more you lift her up the higher you will go. But if I'm only thinking about myself and I never consider her desire to go and grow, the relationship will be one-sided.

Look for him to say great things about you and to be concerned about your goals and desire to reach the plan that God has placed in your life.

Here is your secret just between me and you. Proverbs 4: 6,8 and 9 are small keys to pay attention to as to how he treats and values you. These scriptures are speaking of the value of wisdom, however I would like for you to put your name in the places of her and she. This guy will understand that to promote you brings value to him. He will treat you like a queen in front of everyone.

Warning #1

Regardless of the fact of you being born again or not, Satan hates you. You are a threat to him and everything about his agenda. Just because you are ignorant of his devices does not mean that you are not on his hit list—you are. He hates you because you are a human, and he hates all humans. The one thing that he cannot afford for you to do is to get connected to the right people and for sure get with your God-given mate. So this last bit of information is for the latter stages of this journey, or it could even be at any time during this process if you take it on. I'm doing my best to make this book for everyone.

In this place in my life, I really believe that we who are called have to do everything we can to reach people and not be accidentally exclusive to the world by thinking everyone should know what we're talking about and understand things from our perspective. While we must maintain the integrity of the Gospel, we still have to be relatable.

I hope that some of what I have shared is relatable to everyone, because If I'm only reaching out to Christians this becomes exclusive. I discovered near the end of my walk in finding Meriam, a level of attack towards my commitment to see my decision through. It made me realize just how serious the enemy will be in trying to keep you out of God's plan for your life. I realized that if I used any other measuring tool other than the spirit of God as the final approval, I would never had gotten here. This is why I believe it was important for you that are truly ready for change to have made the decision early in this book to give your heart to Christ.

I know now that my common sense would not have worked. God's way of getting the promises too you are by faith. I think it works that way because in this world everything the devil uses to get you off track is by the senses. So God moves us out of that area to be able to direct us to what he has established for us in our future. Someone you may have thought at one time was the right person for you then, may show up right at the time you make the decision to walk this out. If you don't have a new set of standards you could end up going through another bout with the wrong one and waist time and energy on the wrong choice. Even more serious, they could show up after you have gone through the entire process, discovered who God says is the one and then come back into your life. What will you do then?

Guys and ladies, this is how many of us are tricked into taking on wrong relationships and unequal connections. The Bible calls them unequally yoked relationships. That simply means that you are connecting yourself to a person that will hinder you from going where you need to go or doing what you need to do to improve or to see the best that life has to offer you.

I love Meriam, and she is more than what I expected. She is attractive, smart, talented, a wonderful wife, mother, friend and is spiritually mature. In some ways she is older than I am, and you would have to know us a little more to understand that one. I could never have found her on my own. Not because she was not around my life, but because I would have been distracted by too many other things and people at different stages, moments and times in the years leading up to discovering that God's choice for me was her. Sometimes I get a little feeling of shock when thinking about just how easy it would have been for me to have missed her. I think one of the other great benefits to this place God has walked me through is the fact that now I can use these same principles I've learned with the other parts of my life. "Closing your eyes and seeing with your spirit" works with everything. That process itself saved me. Why?

Because when I was tested before, during and at the very end I had one thing that I could hold on to that kept me on track: I knew without a doubt what God had said. I don't know who you are, and I don't know why you're reading this book, but I do know that what I'm saying to you can keep you out of a lot of troubled stuff. Remember, I'm no expert. All I can do is give you as good of an account of this wonderful experience in my life that I would love for you to experience as well. No two situations are the same, but I'm sure of one thing, and that's that God wants to help you.

Finding your wife and choosing your husband is too important of a decision to do it on your own. Remember, that's been the process you've used up until now. It is your decision to do this whole relationship process differently.

You can use a dating website or friends setting you up or seeing who's at the bar or club or even your parents, but if I were you I'd let God do it for you. For those of you who said, "I thought God Helped me the last time", I hope this experience helps you to realize that the last time was not God at all, but your own senses wrapped in a religious disguise to get what you wanted in the flesh. We can do a great job at fooling ourselves.

Warning #2

During my years as a single man, I had an interesting event that would occur from time to time. It seems the closer I got to Meriam, the more I would get these "words" from people around me declaring who they felt was my wife. The funny thing is, God seemed to be telling everyone else about my wife but not telling me. At one time, I had three different situations near the same time where I was being told that someone was saying to me that God had confirmed to them that they were or someone they knew was my wife. I guess you could say I was lucky in that there were more than one because the fact that there was more than one told me somebody was wrong.

As a desire to get the relationship deal right and to make sure you are in God's will, you must understand the nature of God. God desires to speak to you personally. Sure, there are times when a word or message is given to a Pastor or leader in the body of Christ and maybe even someone close to your life. However, my greatest instances of communication for my life have come directly from God Himself.

I had gone to a music workshop and I had a member of the church I was attending to ride with me. She was a very nice person and I had gotten to know her and her family very well. On this particular day at this workshop the session stopped for a bit for all the attendees to regroup. She and I talked for a moment and then we got up to go to our respective sessions. A person out of the blue walked up to me that I did not know and said, "Did you know that's your wife you were just talking to?" I said, "No, I didn't know that." I just thanked them for the word and went on. I did not tell the young lady what the person said because that was the last thing I needed. I was still waiting for God. I decided that I would not stop anything I was doing to continue to walk with God, and I decided that I would not do anything differently related to that young lady. I felt that they would meet me down the road of life as I continued to seek God for my purpose and His plan for me. It was not the last time that would happen but thank God I waited to hear from God Himself.

Listen, the decision to enter into marriage is far too great a decision to place in someone else's hands. Even your parents and those who are very important to you should be respected and honored by you giving them your attention; however, the journey you will take will not be traveled by anyone but you. Once you make the call to enter into the long-term relationship, you will have to walk it out yourself.

I'm reminded of my days as a high school athlete being recruited during my senior year. I was recruited by all the SEC schools as well as schools as far away as Kansas and even USC in California to come and play for them. I used to get a call from Coach Bear Bryant on Thursday nights, because he would call recruits on that night knowing they had to be home by a certain time. It was a great time in my life, and I have great memories of those experiences. The one thing that sticks out to me, however, that I remember about that time more than anything else is this, my Dad sat me down and said to me that it was my decision to make. He said that if he or anyone else made the decision for me and times got tough, then I would have someone else to blame if they didn't go as I wanted or planned. He said, "This needs to be your decision, son, because it's going to be you that has to make it work, and you don't need anyone else's decision to be responsible for you being in that situation."

This is the point I'm making to you who are reading this. Hear and respect people; however, remember that you want to make this decision yourself, and you want to make it based wholly on God directing you to that person as well as your heart. It should be a decision you and God make together and not anyone else. My dad knew that he wouldn't be with me in the summer running sprints, nor would he be with me when I had to earn my place on the team. It was going to have to be me to make it through the tough times, and that's true for you. There will be tough times as there will be in all areas of your life, but as it is related to marriage, you want to be there because you love that person and they're the one God has endorsed. When those two things are in place, you can know you made the decision on your own and God will be with you to help you as you walk it out.

"The Waiting's Most Valuable Player"

This is my story. You will have yours, and it will most likely be totally different. No two stories are the same. There was a lot of time between these occurrences I've shared, and no doubt there was a lot of waiting involved. I can't say that I've captured it all, but I do believe that I've captured the key elements which made a difference in me being able to navigate my way through the rough areas with God's help. If I had a most valuable trophy to give out for the years leading up to now, it would no doubt take a big table to hold them all. However, there's one I have to talk about during the waiting points.

Anybody that knows Nettie Barnes understands clearly what I'm about to say. Not only as a married person, but as a Christian single, there is nothing more important than having a mature, no-nonsense, hold-you-accountable person in your life. I guess the thing that was so interesting about Mrs. Barnes was the fact that everything that came out of her mouth was about the Word of God. There were no emotional stances coming from Mrs. Barnes. I started out taking Mrs. Barnes out for lunch, because I didn't want to take anyone else out thinking that it was more than just lunch! Mrs. Barnes kept me on track. I know that there were times when I just felt like giving up and letting the process go. The process of growing and changing is not easy. The process of wanting to just say, "Forget it!" will happen. The feeling that this is taking too long, and having thoughts of "I don't even know if this is going to work" will come in to get you to lose your hope. Just remember, "faith is the substance of things hoped for but the evidence of things not seen," so your level of commitment will always be tested. In some very difficult times and just when I needed someone to say with me, "Yeah! Man this thing ain't working!" I had Mrs. Nettie Barnes.

You know sometimes you try things out on folks before you pull the trigger and make decisions. You think that what you really want is for someone to say "You're right, man, you need to do something else"! Mrs. Barnes would say, "Well, you might as well just keep on doing what God told you! We not gone do anything but just keep doing that Word!!" You know God has done too much stuff with you for you to start doing anything different now!" She was my Spiritual Life Coach. You see, quitting on God's plans has never, ever, been an option in her life. Without saying it, she was saying, "You are God's. and you and are doing something special, and you can't quit now." She has been my cheerleader and fan club, teacher and friend. If you ever see me on some ministry platform and you see some well-dressed women with a prayer hanky in her hand, you'll know that is my fiends is Mrs. Nettie Barnes. Her sidekick is a lady named Lola Carter; she is a tough prayer warrior too. With these two backing me up and praying for me, I knew I was covered in the blood. Find a good, solid mature covering related to your waiting period. You will still need a pastor and a church, but this is during the times you're not at church. This is related to everyday life.

"CONCLUSION"

Here's my final point for you. Every phase of life has challenges, and your life will always be tested. My greatest reward in life is my family. I'm proud of all four of my children (and the 5th one, a teenager we recently were blessed with), and I'm extremely proud of my wife Meriam. I've heard it said that you can tell a lot about a person by who they marry. I'm not saying that that's the gospel, but I'm thinking that if you judge me by marrying Meriam, then I should look pretty good. Even with all that said, relationships and marriage is still a process of growth, maturity, challenge and compromise. My greatest strength regarding my relationship with Meriam comes from knowing that God gave her to me. I found her with the help of the Spirit of God, and I believe she chose me by the same Spirit.

This book was not a bunch of do's and don'ts, and not a list of scriptures that you can just place into your life to try and duplicate what you have seen in my life. You shouldn't look to recreate the same scenarios in your life. But this was an example of how God spoke to me and guided me in the direction of His choice for me. It's not only WHAT He said, but also HOW He spoke to me in a unique way to fit my personality and level of understanding to get me here. This is why you should get to know God. Because this is what the relationship with God is all about. His reference point to communicate with you is his Word, and He uses it to show you great and wonderful things that are already in place for you to receive.

There's an old saying "What you don't know can't hurt you," but we all know that's not true. What I didn't know kept me away from Meriam, and learning to love God got me to her and has opened my life up to a whole lot more. Until you learn to love Him, you'll never know how to love anyone else.

I pray you learn to love God as well, because He already loves you,

Be blessed!

Byron P. Franklin Sr.

ACKNOWLEDGMENTS

Max and Bobbie Miller

There was this crazy meeting of two of the most unlikely people in my life that I'm going to start out thanking. In Fairfield, Alabama, one Sunday at First Baptist Church, I had decided to stand at the door and great people. Most of the congregation were up in years and really needed a little help coming up the steps, so I decided to make that my ministry. One Sunday morning as I did my normal greeting, a white couple got out of their car and began to walk inside. I said to myself, "These folks have got to be lost." I had come to this conclusion because we were in the middle of an all-black community, and as we all know, Sunday is the most segregated time of the week. I was prepared to help them with directions, and I was sure that when they realized that the church was all black that they would quickly turn and head back out. I greeted them and said, "Good morning!! The guy said "Hello, I'm Max and this is Bobbie and we're coming to church." I said, "Are ya'll from Birmingham? He said, "No I'm here on business, and we decided we wanted to go to church this morning, so we just looked in the phone book and picked one." Realizing that they were really intending to come in, I said that I would take them with me into my Sunday school class, and we went in. Not only did they stay through Sunday school, but they also stayed for church. Max was a corn farmer from Illinois and was on a sales trip meeting with Golden Flake. The only thing I could think was, "He must sell a lot of corn." Somehow, we've never lost contact. He and Bobbie would come visit, and we would have lunch each time they would come in town. I was single at the time, and when I would talk to Max he would always talk about the importance of three things:

1. Time.
2. Family
3. God.

They are really up in years now, and of all things, we keep in touch now by good old Facebook. Max came into my life at a time when I think I needed a little push from an outside source to get back into the marriage arena. His message to me was that I was wasting time, and it's so funny that the one thing I wish I could do differently as it relates to Meriam. I would have married sooner. Max, you were right! It had to have been God to bring those two people into our lives. He has a huge family with plenty of grandchildren up in Illinois, but I will always love them for being a part of my life in such a special way.

"Time can get away from you if you're not careful."
-Max Miller

Grace Lindsey

One day years ago, I knew I was in trouble in life and needed help. I was working on my spiritual growth. However, I was struggling with being single and starting over emotionally, and I had a counseling agency number in my pocket and decided to call and make an appointment. The only thing I remember about that day was I felt I needed help right then. I dialed the number, and the person on the other end answered and said, "This is Grace." I laughed and said, "Man! I really need grace right now!"...referring to God's grace. I was thinking later, "Well, that had to be God!!"

Grace Lindsey was her name, and we became very good friends. I have no idea where she is now, but I know that if she had not been there that day, my life may have had a totally different outcome. Thanks, Grace, for being of great help to me in my life at a critical time. I think I became her counselor, and we would laugh about life and really have some great discussions that helped me. Thanks, Grace!

Joe Ciampi

Former Auburn University Head Women's Basketball Coach

I'm not sure why he asked me to do it, but being a part of the Auburn Women's Basketball program was one of the greatest sports highlights of my life. But that's not why I'm talking about Joe. My football career was about to end, and I was in recovery from my left knee being reconstructed. I went off to training camp, and by the end of camp that year, I was back home and done with football at the time. For the first several weeks I did nothing but just sit at home, not realizing that I was going through depression. I just sat around all day. I think I went over to go to the training room, and while I sat with my leg on ice, Joe came over to me and said, "Well whatcha going to do now?" I told him I didn't know, and he quickly said, "Why don't you come out and help us?" My first thought was, "I'm not going out there with a bunch of girls," but I went out anyway just to watch them practice. After watching him make at least one player cry and yell at everybody else, I thought, "Hey! I can do this!" and so I did. Two SEC titles later and two national championship games later, I was part of the winningest programs I'd ever been in. I learned a lot about coaching from Joe, but I learned a lot more about leadership. You would think that this was enough for me to be thanking him, but that's not why Joe is being listed here. Joe Ciampi is responsible for me graduating from Auburn. Getting involved with that program gave me the reason I needed to get up and get going again. Oh, I'd like to believe that I was going to get it back together and move on with my life and realize that I had folks that were counting on me. I do believe that; however, I also realize now that I was at a critical place that many fail to recover from. The opportunity to get involved with one of the greatest women's basketball programs of that time was just the right thing to keep me from falling off the table but even more so, it gave me something that filled some much needed space in my life until God became the main focus for me in my life. Thanks, Joe!

"The team is more important than the individual. If you keep the one who will not follow the team and is always out of order, you lose the team."

Coach Joe Ciampi

SPIRITUAL MENTORS

Dr. Robert G. Twyman was the Pastor of First Baptist Church of Fairfield, Alabama, during the years I actually began the transition from religion to relationship in God. Although our communication has been small over the last 15 years, his impact on my life stands as a part of the initial foundation of ministry work I'm involved in, and I will always stand on. Thanks, Pastor and Mimi.

"Never invite yourself up front, always be invited."
Dr. Robert Twyman

Mrs. Nettie Barnes

Nettie Barnes was my Sunday school teacher who has had one of the most profound effects on my life. If there's any such thing as a spiritual father, then I would have to say that she has to be my spiritual mom. I'll speak of her in the book, but just to add to whatever has been said, Mrs. Barnes was critical to what God has done with me at the most important time in my spiritual life, which was at the beginning. She is still one of my most trusted spiritual mentors/ Moms. Thank you, Mrs. Barns.

"Your arms are too short to box with God."

Apostle Michael D. Moore
Sr. Pastor and Founder of Faith Chapel Christian Center
Co-founder, Visionary Overseer, for Living Word Church

Outside of my natural father, this man has had such a profound impact on my life. A man of character and integrity and one of the greatest teachers this side of heaven. I've talked about him in several places but he and his wife Kennetha, or Pete as she is called, are two very special people. Some people you just can't describe, you have to experience.

Thank you Pastor and Mrs. Pete

"I have seven things…" he would say in every message.

MY FAMILY

Parents

I'll begin with my parents, Milton and Ida Franklin, who have been the greatest parents anyone could have. I always tell the joke that I've raised them well, but of course, that's a joke. The truth is, I can't say enough about the example they set for my sister and I, and I have to say that they are parents to way more than just the two of us. It's a great thing to be able to say that your dad is the greatest man you know. To Tommy and Florence Spencer, the two of you have been such wonderful parents to me and our family, You have opened your home and your hearts in such a profound way and we have been so blessed by you both. We love you very much and thanks for being such great parents.

BYRON P. FRANKLIN, SR.

My children

Byron Jr. and Kelsie were the two primary reasons that this book has happened. My goal was to do whatever I could to give the two of them the right picture of marriage. After giving them the wrong picture, I wanted to do everything I could to help them realize that marriage can work. Guys, I love you and still have the greatest respect for the two of you. You have grown to be adults with a great future ahead, and I pray God leads you into the path He has for the both of you. With Him as the main foundation of your lives ther is nothing you cannot do.

Brandon, Bradley and Craig

Brandon and Bradley The two of you are a direct result of God bringing your mom and I together. I am blessed to be part of your lives and am so looking forward to seeing what God has planned for you. You are both so gifted and a blessing. Craig thank you for allowing Meriam and I the honor of parenting you as a part of this family. You can do whatever you set your mind to and we are expecting great things for you in God.

CPSIA information can be obtained
at www.ICGtesting.com
Printed in the USA
LVHW03s0200101018
592998LV00010B/49/P